Praise for *Listening When Parts Speak*

"Tamala's personal examples are compelling and courageous, and the case studies perfectly illustrate the concepts. People will be able to do considerable work on themselves by trying the exercises, and many IFS therapists will assign this book to clients as an adjunct to the therapy."

— from the foreword by **Richard C. Schwartz, Ph.D.**, founder of Internal Family Systems Therapy

"*Listening When Parts Speak* is an ancestral playbook for unlocking the heart of your wounds and the embodied power of your healing. With beautiful vulnerability and potency, Tamala Floyd offers rich medicine that can only be consumed when a person is genuinely ready and willing to be with the dark fears in the corners of their mind and release the terrorizing burdens in the belly of their pain. For those who are ready, I urge you to let Tamala be your unflinching guide on this journey called healing."

— **Jamari Michael White**, ancestral medicine practitioner

"I would like to thank Tamala Floyd's ancestors for inspiring and guiding her to write this book. As a teacher for over 30 years and an IFS trainer for 20 years, I am extremely impressed with the pedagogy illustrated by Tamala's writing. Her clarity in teaching—first through authentic personal story, followed by theory, case example, meditation, and journal prompts, and finishing with suggestions for anchoring the learning—was nothing short of brilliant. A must-read for all those wanting to enhance their IFS experience and deepen their relationship with ancestors."

— **Ann L. Sinko, LMFT**, senior IFS trainer

"From the profound wisdom of the ancestors to the depths of our hearts and minds, *Listening When Parts Speak* is a beautiful blend of personal reflections, heartfelt meditations, and transformative insights. With loving ancestral guidance, Tamala invites readers on a journey of self-discovery and inner healing using the Internal Family Systems model. *Listening When Parts Speak* rises as essential reading for anyone seeking to explore their inner world and uncover the truest expression of themselves. Thank you, Ancestors! Thank you, Tamala!"

— **Crystal R. Jones, LCSW**, Internal Family Systems Institute lead trainer and consultant and founder of Life Source Counseling Center, Inc.

"I highly recommend *Listening When Parts Speak* to everyone, regardless of your level of understanding of IFS and/or Ancestral Healing. Tamala introduces the reader to both modalities in a clear and understandable way. She then translates the teaching into meditations and exercises that support the reader applying the concepts to their own system. Tamala generously shares her personal journey with IFS and ancestor work in a moving and inspiring way. I encourage you all to read this powerful book and experiment with Tamala's meditations and exercises. *Listening When Parts Speak* is an incredible tool that can impact our own internal exploration and our work with our clients."

— **Pamela K. Krause, LCSW**, senior lead trainer for IFS-I

"In *Listening When Parts Speak*, Tamala's expertise and profound commitment to Internal Family Systems shine through every page. She guides readers with an incredibly nurturing touch and a compassionate approach for anyone seeking to embark on or continue their path toward growth, self-respect, and self-fulfillment. Tamala has created a sanctuary within these pages letting readers know that not only do their feelings matter but they hold the key to deep healing. This book is a mastery of a holistic mind-and-soul approach; it can be a wonderful companion on the journey toward self-love as well as a fantastic guide on the inner workings of IFS."

— **Lorriane Anderson**, spiritual teacher, author of the best-selling *The Witch's Apothecary*, and co-author of the best-selling Seasons of the Witch oracle deck series

"Tamala Floyd's book deepens and expands our connection and understanding with 'parts' of ourselves through IFS and support from our ancestors, delicately peeling back the layers of life with clarity and wisdom through her personal stories. The book is filled with inspiring meditations of healing and journal exercises, uncovering the power of self-leadership. Tamala leads us in processing trauma and pain to get in touch with sources of strength, creativity, compassion, and connection to recognize our own true Spirit. You'll come away with tools to navigate life with wisdom and intuition. A must-read for anyone seeking a holistic approach to healing and self-discovery."

— **Jataunia Schweitzer, MMTCP,**
certified mindfulness meditation teacher

"It's a privilege to recommend *Listening When Parts Speak*. Tamala, who has rich experience as a licensed clinical social worker and therapist, beautifully integrates the principles of Internal Family Systems Therapy with the wisdom of our ancestors. Using her extensive expertise and stories from her own healing journey, Tamala makes the exploration of complex therapeutic concepts approachable and deeply engaging. Tamala's narratives, practical exercises, and meditations highlight the path of IFS and ancestral healing, making it accessible to all. Tamala's ability to effectuate growth and understanding makes this a valuable resource for therapists, clients, and anyone dedicated to their personal discovery and healing path."

— **Lisa R. Savage, LCSW**, and **Kim L. Knight, LMHC**, founders of Clinicians of Color, LLC

"Through ancestral wisdom, we are invited alongside Tamala as she befriends and heals parts of herself, teaching us IFS in the process. This book is unlike other IFS books out there—it offers refreshing guidance on healing intergenerational trauma with the support of our ancestors. Each meditation is a gift offering a chance of self-discovery and connection with our ancestors and with our parts. This is a joy to read and will inspire curiosity and provide healing for many generations to come."

— **Daphne Fatter, Ph.D.**, certified IFS licensed psychologist, IFS clinical consultant, certified ancestral lineage healing practitioner

"Listen and heal! Tamala Floyd has created a gem that will help many people heal for years to come. Using her meditations, I was able to reach and identify deeply rooted trauma that had been suppressed for years. As a result, I'm on a healing journey and see myself in different ways. As I develop relationships with my Parts, giving them a voice and listening to what they have to say will allow me to clear paths and move forward. *Listening When Parts Speak* will become an essential resource in my life."

— **Theresa R. Glaspie**, counseling client

Listening When Parts Speak

Listening When Parts Speak

A Practical Guide to Healing with Internal Family Systems Therapy and Ancestor Wisdom

TAMALA FLOYD, LCSW

HAY HOUSE LLC
Carlsbad, California • New York City
London • Sydney • New Delhi

Published in the United States by: Hay House LLC: www.hayhouse.com® • ***Published in Australia by:*** Hay House Australia Pty Ltd: www.hayhouse.com.au • ***Published in the United Kingdom by:*** Hay House UK Ltd: www.hayhouse.co.uk • ***Published in India by:*** Hay House Publishers (India) Pvt Ltd: www.hayhouse.co.in

Cover design: Kathleen Lynch
Interior design: Julie Davison
Indexer: Shapiro Indexing Services

Cataloging-in-Publication Data is on file at the Library of Congress

Tradepaper ISBN: 978-1-4019-7565-4
E-book ISBN: 978-1-4019-7566-1
Audiobook ISBN: 978-1-4019-7567-8

10 9 8 7 6 5 4 3 2 1
1st edition, August 2024

Printed in the United States of America

SFI label applies to the text stock

This product uses responsibly sourced papers and/or recycled materials. For more information, see www.hayhouse.com.

To the wise and intuitive women of my

mother's mother's line, especially

Marva L. Collins Bush (my mom).

The guided meditations in *Listening When Parts Speak* are available as free audio recordings. To access the recordings, please visit www.hayhouse.com/download and enter the Product ID **5654** and the Download Code **audio.**

Please listen to the meditations at a time when you can relax and when you won't be interrupted. Never listen to them while driving or engaging in activities where you need to be alert.

If you need assistance in accessing the recordings, please contact Hay House Customer Care by phone—US (800) 654-5126 or INTL CC+(760) 431-7695—or visit www.hayhouse.com/contact.

Contents

Foreword

I'm honored to write the foreword for this powerful, groundbreaking book. Its author, Tamala Floyd, in addition to being a Self-led person and terrific writer, is our first Black Internal Family Systems trainer. For probably 30 of the 40 years I've been developing IFS, the community was embarrassingly white. I'm so grateful for pioneers like Percy Ballard, Deran Young, and Tamala, who persisted despite hurtful slights they endured from us, until we took seriously the need to educate ourselves to become more racially sensitive. To my delight, the IFS community is quite diverse now because of the efforts of charismatic leaders like Tamala.

And now she's contributing this wonderful book, which I love for several reasons. First, traditionally the IFS Institute has focused on training therapists who would then bring IFS to their clients. Recently we have been wanting to find ways to bring it directly to the public, and this book does that beautifully. The format of describing an IFS concept, following that with a personal example followed by a case example and then exercises, is very clear and user-friendly. Tamala's personal examples are compelling and courageous, and the case studies perfectly illustrate the concepts. People will be able to do considerable work on themselves by trying the exercises, and many IFS therapists will assign this book to clients as an adjunct to the therapy.

Second, I have been wanting the spiritual side of IFS to be more accessible and took a first step in that direction in my last book, *No Bad Parts*. Tamala takes a bold second step by combining IFS with a system called ancestral medicine healing. I have been working with ancestral spirits for many years but haven't described that work for fear of IFS being written off as "woo-woo." In the relatively early days of IFS's development, I discovered that some of the burdens that parts carried had nothing to do with their lived experiences. Instead, they had been passed down through generations and came from traumas that were decades or centuries old. I called these *legacy burdens*, and unburdening them has become a big part of the IFS process.

Over the past several decades, I and many other IFS therapists have found that the spirits of clients' relatives would come to them spontaneously during sessions. After getting my skeptical parts to relax, I found those spirits to be very helpful guides for navigating clients' inner and outer lives; and they also provided clients with valuable qualities we came to call *heirlooms*. Now that IFS is so widespread and popular, I am emboldened to speak more openly about that kind of work and am grateful to Tamala for offering such a clear path to it, with beautiful examples and descriptions. I encourage you to work with parts who might be allergic to anything spiritual so you can experience the abundant gifts that this book offers, many of which do not relate to spirituality. You don't have to believe in the otherworldly to benefit enormously from this book.

Finally, because of Tamala's extensive experience working with BIPOC clients, this book fills a void in the IFS literature. The case examples offer a window into common struggles of people of color and how to unload legacy burdens like that of the Strong Black Woman, the roots of which lie in slavery. Tamala's rich prose brings both her personal and case vignettes to life.

This book is destined to become a classic in the IFS community and, I hope and expect, in the self-help and psychotherapy worlds too. I'm so grateful for all the riches in it and for all of Tamala's many contributions to our community.

— **Richard C. Schwartz, Ph.D.**, founder
of Internal Family Systems Therapy

CHAPTER 1

The Ancestors and Internal Family Systems Therapy

I sit across the table from my friend and colleague Daphne enthralled, listening to her words with my whole body. My skin absorbs her excitement. I feel my heart opening and expanding. My mind full of questions and my voice ready to engage the conversation fully. I find what she's sharing riveting, unbelievable, and resonant. Daphne shares in hushed tones, not wanting the diners around us to overhear, how her connection with her ancestors through a process called ancestral lineage healing is helping her through a tough divorce. "I know this sounds woo-woo," she says. But she can't deny the miraculous impact of her ancestors' expression of love through guidance, support, advice, and care.

She goes on to talk about the synchronicity and alignment of people brought into her life at exactly the right time to assist her since the beginning of her ancestral healing journey. She shares her experiences with such conviction that a part of me wants to sign up immediately. However, a part that holds skepticism thinks, "How can dead people you've never met help you in your life? This is a load of crap!"

I spent the greater part of my adult life seeking my own healing from childhood trauma and professionally supporting others in their healing as a psychotherapist and coach. I watched firsthand as my friend Daphne healed using the knowledge, wisdom, and support of her loving ancestors. The combination of my unfolding research on ancestral lineage healing, my ongoing search for personal healing, and my commitment to championing the healing of others satisfied the skeptical part. She—the skeptical part—came to understand the importance of this work. As the part of me that was initially leery relaxed, I began my ancestral healing journey.

MY BEGINNINGS WITH IFS AND ANCESTOR WISDOM

I had that foreshadowing conversation with Daphne when she and I were working together as program assistants on a training held by the organization Black Therapists Rock to introduce Black therapists to Internal Family Systems Therapy—the modality I specialized in, which was viewed as a game-changer in the fields of psychotherapy and trauma healing. I had come to Internal Family Systems (IFS) first as a student, then as a client, and in the course of my own healing discovered it allowed access to my internal psyche that was not previously available. I sought treatment for years for childhood traumas, but I didn't receive healing until I discovered IFS. When I did, I gained an awareness that I am not of one mind, but composed of multiple minds or subpersonalities. Before IFS therapy, I thought I was the one who held the pain and experiences of my traumas. I came to understand that the subpersonalities or parts were the wounded ones, and I also had parts who were not affected by the traumas. IFS applied language and steps to what I intuitively knew but couldn't quite prove: we all already have what we need to heal. With my clients, my job is to help them gain access to their healing potential.

Another instrumental component in my healing journey was ancestor healing work. My conversation with Daphne stirred a desire in me to build relationships with my own ancestors. I began working with an ancestral medicine healing practitioner to not only build relationships but also heal generational trauma on multiple ancestral family lines and receive the intergenerational gifts of these lines. Through the healing practices of IFS and ancestral medicine, I have created enduring relationships with my parts and ancestors, who continue to support me in my daily life and all its challenges.

My personal experience with these two healing modalities informed my practice with clients. I immediately shifted to providing IFS therapy exclusively, because I knew it was the best way to treat significant trauma and to achieve positive shifts in a shorter period. I describe IFS to my clients as a therapy that gets to the root of the problem instead of treating symptoms. Clients aren't simply being taught how to cope; they experience deep healing. Healing shifts the entire system, allowing clients to move through the world and their lives in ways that were unavailable to them before IFS therapy.

When I learned about IFS, I had been treating a primarily Black female clientele, as well as other women of color, some white women, and some male clients, for over 20 years. My areas of expertise include childhood sexual abuse, molestation, and physical abuse, and I have witnessed the pain Black women in particular carry with these histories. They are unduly burdened with beliefs and feelings of irreparable brokenness, worthlessness, never feeling good enough or lovable; additionally, they carry the pain of stolen innocence, abandonment, rejection, otherness, and aloneness. This results in self-blame to make sense of what happened to them, or a quest for perfection to compensate for what happened, or acceptance of demeaning and humiliating treatment by themselves and others to recreate the familiar.

As a Black woman, I find that a notable difference in working with Black women clients as compared to my other clients is an immediate comfort and feeling of safety. I'm not sure if this is related to the kinship shared between Black folks, but I believe that's part of it. On many occasions I've been told, "My body relaxed when I found out you were Black," or "I don't have to explain and defend my Black experiences with you," or "It feels safe to share my abuse with another Black woman," or "I'm not bracing for your response as I've done with white therapists." I share this for two reasons: first, to acknowledge the profound impact of receiving healing from someone who looks like you, and second, to bring attention to the inherent extra burden carried by Black clients who have white therapists. I believe it is the therapist's responsibility to address the obvious differences early on, keep the lines of communication open around the topic of race, and to own their blind spots throughout the therapeutic relationship.

WHAT IS INTERNAL FAMILY SYSTEMS THERAPY?

Internal Family Systems (IFS) therapy was developed by Dr. Richard Schwartz through his work with eating-disordered adolescents in the 1980s. He found that his clients spoke about "parts" of themselves, and as he began to understand from his clients how parts operate within our internal system, he discovered that we *all* have parts; it is the norm, not the exception. Dr. Schwartz learned that clients had internal conversations with their parts and could get separation from their parts and the parts' extreme behavior. When separation occurred, he found, clients became calm, curious, and nonjudgmental. *Self* is the term he used to describe this calm center, this deep essence at the core of every person. Within the internal system—essentially an internal "family"—Self acts as a wise, compassionate leader able to heal and lead.[1] The goals of IFS therapy, as stated in the classic work on the model by Richard Schwartz and Martha Sweezy, are to liberate parts from their extreme roles, restore Self-leadership, create balance and harmony within the system, and to bring Self-energy to the external world.[2]

Achieving the goals of IFS therapy gives us access to a wealth of life-changing benefits. When we liberate our parts from their extreme roles, they are less reactive, which increases our options of choice and improves relationships. In addition, we can access their innate wisdom as advisors. The restoration of Self-leadership means Self is at the head of our internal system. When parts trust Self to lead, they are open to its help when they get activated; they can relax, allowing Self to make decisions and choices in the best interests of the entire system. For example, when a frustrated part trusts Self, it will share the cause of its upset with Self and, instead of acting out of its frustration, allow

Self to speak on its behalf. The more trust between parts and Self, the greater access parts have to Self as a supportive leader, increasing the balance and harmony within the system. We feel more comfortable and present in our body when Self leads instead of our parts. We can bring more Self-energy to the external world when we are grounded in the present and accept that everyone has parts and not personalize the poor behavior of others.

WHAT IS ANCESTRAL LINEAGE HEALING?

In my quest to learn about ancestral lineage healing, I found several definitions I'd like to share with you. The practitioner I eventually sought out and continue to work with, Jamari White, defines ancestral lineage healing as follows: "Ancestral lineage healing is a ritual practice of cultivating conscious, vibrant connection with your ancestors to heal intergenerational trauma, and reclaim and embody centuries of lost ancestral wisdom and guidance."[3] It's that last part about accessing lost wisdom that intrigued and propelled me forward. In Daniel Foor's book, *Ancestral Medicine: Rituals for Personal and Family Healing,* I learned the benefits of connecting and being in relationship with ancestors to heal generational trauma. Foor says, "Ancestral lineage healing is a specific approach to relating directly with wise and loving lineage ancestors for the purposes of personal, family and cultural healing." I was most drawn to this approach because of the multidimensional healing benefits.[4] Foor outlines how relating to ancestors supports psychological and physical health, heals intergenerational family dysfunction, and culturally transforms historical and collective trauma.[5]

My personal experiences with ancestor healing practices increased my trust in the wisdom of our ancestors.

I started using my ancestor-inspired meditations with clients (more about how I developed the meditations later). As I guided them through these meditations, they shared a knowing and familiar connection with their ancestors that enhanced their experience of healing. The presence of ancestors in the healing journey, I discovered, helps clients feel supported, understood, and loved. Many clients had never connected with ancestors and their wisdom prior to being introduced to my meditations. I encouraged them to invite their ancestors into their daily lives and into the therapy process, and to consult with them on decisions and challenges. My clients found the new relationship beneficial and yearned to stay connected so they could learn more about and from their ancestors.

I also brought ancestors into the IFS healing process through legacy burden work, which I'll describe in Chapter 11. It made sense to me, when working with traumas inherited from generational lines, that ancestors need to actively participate in the healing process. Some of the burdens passed down to my Black female clients in particular are self-reliance; the need to be strong while denying vulnerability or emotions; striving and feeling guilty for resting; a scarcity perspective believing that there's not enough and if they stop pushing they will miss out; caretaking others and ignoring self-care; sexualization of Black women and girls; colorism; racism; and of course slavery, which is the origin of many of these legacy burdens. Ancestors have an understanding about the burdens of their line and can contribute immensely to clearing its generational burdens. Inviting the ancestors to do the work of releasing the burdens, while clients observe the process, has resulted in remarkable transformations for the clients. In this process, ancestors also let the client know the gifts or heirlooms of the line and share them with the client. A few of the heirlooms of Black ancestral lines are family loyalty, a broad definition of family including "aunties" and "cousins" based on connection in addition to blood ties, family traditions, rituals and celebrations, common sense, instinct for survival, innovation, and traditional healing. I have found that inviting the ancestors to lead the unburdening process, allowing them to do the work with the ancestral line, results in a fuller, more complete release of the burdens and a deep connection between the client and their ancestral line.

My first session with Jamari started with an assessment of the health of each of my primary ancestral lines: mother's mother's, mother's father's, father's mother's, and father's father's line. This assessment revealed that my mother's mother's line was the healthiest and the one I felt the closest to. I decided to begin to get to know the ancestors in my mother's mother's lineage.

When I met my Ancestor Guide on my mother's mother's side, she showed up tall, dark, dancing expressively with her long limbs, dressed in brightly colored yellows and oranges. Seeing her brought both joy and sadness. Joy for how well and unburdened she appeared and sadness because I, too, wished to experience the lightness of an unburdened life. I asked her for a blessing for my sadness. Her body began to move rhythmically. Although there was no music, her movements were melodic. Her hands came together at her heart several times. I interpreted what she was doing as dancing and praying. She gently corrected my impression by saying, "The dance is the prayer."

My guide turned her attention to the healing of my unwell ancestors. She held a quilt in her hands and waved it around to capture them. Each unwell ancestor landed on a square of the quilt that represented their unwellness and became one with the quilt.

I tried to share what was happening with Jamari, but the words got caught in my throat. When I attempted to speak a second time, the sound was choked back. "No need to speak to me, just be with your ancestor," Jamari suggested gently.

I asked my Ancestor Guide, "Are you the one who takes my voice away?" Around that time, I was frequently losing my voice while working with clients, as often as once a week. In the middle of a session, I would get a lump in my throat that only the smallest bit of sound could move past. I'd drink water, suck throat lozenges, clear my throat, and cough, but nothing loosened the lump. I even had to end a few sessions early, motioning to my client that I couldn't speak.

"Yes, I am the one," my guide said. She explained that she does it to help me slow down, rest, and be. I got a sense that I would soon use my voice in a new way. She invited me into relationship with her through connecting regularly and using my hands. Lastly, she told me that the gifts of this line are peace, wisdom, artful use of the hands, and uncomplicated living.

At one point in the session, I felt an explosion of pain on the right front side of my head. She said this happens when I won't let things go. I realized she was right; I was trying to control the process instead of allowing it to happen. She suggested that I just be. When I allowed myself to be present without the need to control, her presence intensified, and the headache subsided, replaced with a sense of peace and calm. I had experienced unbearable migraine headaches since college and undergone many treatments with varying degrees of relief. My wise ancestor gave me an age-old antidote: stop controlling, allow, and be.

My dancing ancestor visited me in my dreams for the next two nights. She did not speak. She danced. I was drawn into her dance, unable to take my eyes off her. I was reminded of her words, "The dance is the prayer," and realized she is praying for me, continually.

ANCESTRAL HEIRLOOMS

One week after my first ancestral lineage healing session, Deran Young, the founder of Black Therapists Rock (BTR), invited me to lead the morning meditation at BTR's first Heirloom Summit: Transforming Legacy Burdens to Legacy Gifts three days later. Though I had no clue what I would do in the meditation, I agreed, and then immediately went online to research meditations that involved legacy burdens and gifts for inspiration. I found a few, but none were what I was looking for. Interestingly, I did not fret, which is what I would have done prior to my ancestral healing session. I had a serene sense that it would work out fine.

A group of ancestors came to me in a dream that night. The dancing ancestor was not one of them. These ancestors knew my need and generously shared a guided imagery meditation. When I had created meditations in the past, I experienced meditation from the outside, as a viewer and creator of what was happening. This time, my ancestors gifted the meditation as a firsthand experience from within the guided imagery. I was the main character. Instead of watching the meditation unfold, I was inside the meditation, experiencing it visually, tactilely, fragrantly, emotionally, auditorily. The dreamer and the dreamed merged. In my over 30 years of meditating, it was the most vibrant, tangible, and heartfelt experience I have ever had.

When I woke, I knew this was the Summit meditation. I transcribed it with the guidance of my ancestors, who stood close behind me. They provided gentle nudges for correction when I got an idea or word wrong. At times, they assisted me in re-experiencing the meditation to truly capture the essence. The significance of my ancestors gifting me with the meditation for a Summit on Legacy Burdens and Legacy Gifts is not lost on me. I am immensely grateful to them for showing up when I had no idea what I would do a mere three days before the event.

The meditation wasn't the only gift I received that night. They declared that this meditation would be included in a book of IFS-inspired guided imagery meditations that I would eventually publish. They went on to assure me that they will assist me every step of the way. I was instructed that I should not distribute the meditations in written or recorded form yet—I should save them for the book—but I could lead people through them verbally. My excitement brimmed over, as this felt so deeply in line with my purpose.

The Cabin with the Ancestor meditation went exceptionally well at the Summit. I shared with the group how my ancestors transported me in my dream state to the world where this meditation takes place and supported the transfer of the experience into the written word. The feedback I received included words like *wonderful* and *amazing,* and phrases like *I felt so connected to my ancestors. It felt so real.* I also got many comments expressing gratitude and appreciation for the meditation. One of the most meaningful compliments came when Dr. Richard Schwartz told me he had enjoyed it. "Be sure to remain connected to your ancestors," he said. I was moved by three participants of the training reaching out to request a copy of the meditation, one saying she wanted to use it in an IFS training where she would discuss legacy burdens and the other two hoping to use it to continue the dialogue with their ancestors. Unfortunately, I had to say not yet to the distribution of the meditation; I wanted to honor my ancestors' promise that it would become part of a book.

The night after the success of the Cabin with the Ancestor meditation, my ancestors came to me in a dream proclaiming themselves my Writing Clan. They joined together to assist me in creating nine additional meditations, which you'll find in this book. The Writing Clan came to me in times of rest, usually as I was falling asleep, in the twilight hours prior to waking, during my morning meditation, or as I sat simply being. In those times, as with the first meditation, I entered the world of the meditation with my ancestor guides. The meditation offerings continued for six months. Then, after delivering the meditation I call Labyrinth with the Elders, the Writing Clan went silent. However, I had several meditations already given me that I hadn't transcribed from the notes I always jotted down at the end of the meditation session. Together with the Writing Clan, I completed the unfinished meditations. Although the Clan never explicitly told me we were complete, I knew it intuitively. These are the meditations that make up this book, along with three meditations that were created without the assistance of my ancestors: Qualities of Self, Be With, and Trailblazers.

My dancing ancestor reappeared in my dream that night too. She came to show me that she had started taking my speaking voice as a therapist away to replace it with my written voice, and that I would use my hands in this effort in the same way my ancestors did as quilters, tillers of soil, cultivators of gardens, and crafters of things to sell. The magnificence of this dream is that it showed scenes from the past when I had lost my voice and the ways I would use my written voice in the future. Like a movie, I saw myself in various stages of writing a book, longhand with paper and pen, typing on a laptop, researching, and reading source material. In juxtaposition, my ancestors were displayed across the screen using their hands to create, which clarified the connection between the use of my hands and theirs for creation. I feel a deep kinship with the ancestors of my mother's mother's line, women I never knew personally but know intimately by their significant influence in my life. The dance that night was one of celebration and prayer for my acceptance of the meditations and willingness to transform into a written-word healer.

FOLLOWING ANCESTOR INSPIRATIONS

I want to speak to the importance of adhering to ancestor inspirations. After sharing the Cabin with the Ancestor meditation at the Summit, I went on to share it in IFS Level 1 trainings as I advanced from program assistant to solo lead trainer. Many people who experienced it suggested that I make the meditations available in an audio recording. I had offers of help and suggestions of quick ways to create the audio. I jumped into the project fully.

A consulting client of mine who was a partner in a publishing enterprise wanted to bring me on as an author. I shared my desire to create an audio of the meditations, and she was enthusiastic. I submitted a proposal, but the process stalled multiple times. About six months in I was still without a contract. Finally, my client came to me with the news that she had left the publishing company partnership due to irreconcilable differences. She told me she still believed in the project and offered to pass it on to an editor at Hay House. She made no promises, but she wished me success.

I had a Zoom call with an acquisitions editor at Hay House in September. The editor acknowledged my desire to create an audio but asked if I would consider writing a book instead. I was surprised by this reminder; I had pursued the vision of creating an audio so vigorously that I had lost sight of my ancestors' promise that there would be a book. I said yes, I was definitely interested in writing a book, and immediately started working on a book proposal.

I had followed the audio path because it was what people in the IFS community were requesting. But I didn't hear from the Writing Clan once while I was pursuing the project in audio form. Now my ancestors returned after a year of silence in honor of their word to support my writing process, and together we created a proposal I felt proud of. I pressed Send on the e-mail to the editor on October 12, and 20 days later, I got an e-mail with a subject line that read, "Hay House Offer." At the time, I was on a transatlantic crossing from London back to the United States. I couldn't think of a more beautiful place and time to receive the news.

I share this part of my journey to illuminate the difference between being on purpose with the inspiration of ancestors and acting in my own strength. When I pursued a quick way to get the meditations published that met the needs of my beloved IFS community, the project was stalled with no forward movement and ultimately aborted six months later. When I was in alignment with the inspiration of my ancestors, the first step of their promise of a book was realized in a mere four months after my work first came to the attention of Hay House.

The work of ancestral healing and connection is not magic, although it can feel and appear that way. I liken it to my relationship with my children. As a mom, I worked to meet most of my kids' needs and many of their wants. They did not have to worry about where food, water, electricity, clothes, etc., would come from or if they would come. My husband and I provided for them out of love, responsibility, and care. Our ancestors are the same way. As an attuned parent, I anticipate or see a need and respond; when we connect with our ancestors, they do the same. They love and care about us and what we care about. They support us in cultivating the gifts of our ancestral lines. Just as my ancestors were waiting to connect and assist, yours are too.

What I hope to offer you through the reading of this book is a return to the sacredness of your essential Self to affirm those parts of yourself you had to hide to gain acceptance, love, and care. I hope that through this work you grow to courageously and unapologetically express the whole of who you are. The healing I hope for you will come through the relationships you build with your parts and ancestors. Through the principles, exercises, tools, and meditations, you will learn your internal system. This includes building a trusting relationship with your parts, which will decrease their extreme behaviors and help you discover that you can heal them. I also hope to increase your access to Self by inviting your ancestors into your healing work with you.

SIX ASSUMPTIONS

Richard Schwartz's work on IFS identifies six assumptions that are foundational to the work we'll do together in this book.[6] As you work with your parts, hold each of these assumptions as truth. It will help support you as you get to know your parts.

Assumption 1: We all have parts

The model asserts that we all have parts. I have parts. You have parts. Even if we aren't aware of them, we still have parts. Have you ever had the experience of being of two minds or more on a topic or situation? For example, with the possibility of a job promotion, you may hear a voice say, "You're not qualified; you're not ready." And another says, "You've worked hard and earned this." One part will tell you, show you, and even provide examples from your past about how qualified you are and what you've done to prepare for the promotion. While another part will have a strong stance that you will fail if you take the promotion, and it, too, will give reasons from your past and/or unforeseen future dangers to support why you are not ready. This is an example of how parts may show themselves within your internal system.

Assumption 2: Parts are forced into extreme roles

Parts have been forced into unnatural roles due to attachment wounds and/or trauma. Gina Ryder, an educator and journalist, defines the origin of attachment trauma as "a rupture in the bonding process between a child and their primary caregiver."[7] When our needs are not understood or met as children, or we experience abuse and/or trauma, parts take on extreme roles to protect us from the pain we previously experienced. Our parts may be activated with even the slightest provocation. If a situation is the least bit like the original one, parts will respond with intensity as if they are protecting us from the initial pain. Parts can express themselves extremely through emotions, such as rage or sadness, somatically through migraine headaches or nausea, with images in vivid dreams or horrifying nightmares or through beliefs like "I'm not good enough."

Assumption 3: All parts are welcome

Are all parts welcome? What about parts that hurt people or do bad things? IFS holds that all parts are welcome within an internal system that chooses to understand and get to know each of the parts. It is only through relationship with our parts that we can welcome them. Relationship builds trust. As trust deepens, our parts will share their experiences with us. We welcome our parts by being with them and validating their experiences as they share who they are. We say there are no bad parts. But parts do engage poor strategies to get their needs met.

Assumption 4: We all have a Self

Self is the core or essence of a person. Self is also called the Soul, the Seat of Consciousness, and Prana. Like parts, we all have a Self. It is the intuitive, wise, healing energy we all possess.

Assumption 5: Parts carry burdens

Burdens are emotions, beliefs, and thoughts that affect how parts view themselves, others, and the world, and impact their interactions. Parts are not their burdens; they carry burdens. The extreme roles parts take on are their burdens. Instead of referring to a part as "The Rager," which makes the part the burden, we want to say, a part that has, expresses, feels, or carries rage. This allows for separation between the part and its emotions or actions.

Assumption 6: Parts are well-intentioned

We must always remember that regardless of how parts behave, they are always well-intentioned. Our job is to connect with our parts and get to know them to understand their intentions. Even parts who cause problems and difficulties in our lives have the best intentions. Parts do what they do because they are not aware of their impact or alternatives. They often believe that if they stop, something bad will happen to us or someone important to us.

HOW TO USE THIS BOOK

I wrote *Listening When Parts Speak* to support you on your healing journey. Although I'm a psychotherapist, I realize not everyone chooses therapy as their path to healing. I also realize therapy still carries stigma for some people, including in the Black community and among other people of color. For others, it may not be an option for other reasons. But everyone deserves to heal, and my mission is to use my expertise as a therapist to offer the phenomenal gift of access to the healing resource within you. So, whether you're engaging this work for self-help, as a client in therapy, as a mental health therapist, or as a practitioner/coach, it has transformational potential. Therapists and practitioners can use the book in working with their clients *and* as part of their personal work. Regardless of how the information, meditations, and/or exercises are used, they are not a substitute for therapeutic services. As you begin working with your system and parts, if you get stuck, you find the work too overwhelming or highly triggering, or your symptoms worsen, these are indicators that you would benefit from working with an IFS therapist or practitioner. Please refer to the resources in Chapter 14 to locate an IFS professional.

Each chapter begins with a vignette of my experience working with my own parts. Then I introduce you to key IFS concepts, and in most of the chapters, I include a vignette of working with a client's system that highlights the concepts in the chapter. Most of the client vignettes are a composite of multiple client cases blended and presented as a single case. They include memories of childhood sexual abuse, domestic violence and witnessing violence, suicidal ideation and attempts of suicide, loss of a child, racism and discrimination, vomiting, and sexual trafficking.

At the end of the chapter you'll find a meditation, followed by exercises to anchor the learning and experience. The concepts and meditations build on one another. If you are new to IFS, I suggest reading the book in order. If you have experience with IFS, you may choose the chapter that best meets your needs at a particular time or for a specific situation. Be sure to have a journal or a notebook at hand to track your experiences and growth as you work with your parts.

I wrote this book with the intention that you will meet, get to know, and heal your parts. With that in mind, know that your parts will get activated as you read. This may happen because some parts will resonate with my parts or the parts of my clients while other parts will disagree or be skeptical. This book may activate parts around your unhealed trauma, family and relationship struggles, and myriad other yet-to-be-addressed concerns. My suggestion is to slow down when you notice a strong response to what you're reading, breathe, and pay attention to what is going on in your body. What sensations do you notice? What memories are coming up? What are you thinking? Then journal what comes up for you. There may be times when you have to put the book down to address what's coming up for you, and that's okay. The relationship between you, your parts, and the material of this book is interactive. The more you listen when your parts speak and attend to what they bring to your awareness, the more you're going to gain from the reading of this book.

Self-Help

Therapy and coaching are not required to benefit from this book. It can be used independently as a self-help tool. The teachings, meditations, and exercises help foster trust between the Self and parts, which is essential to the healing process. The IFS concepts, ancestor-inspired meditations, and exercises are to deepen relationship and understanding of your parts, to increase internal and external Self-leadership (meaning Self is in the seat of consciousness), and to connect with the wisdom and guidance of ancestors. Self-leadership involves a shift in your internal system from being reactive and/or passive to being more intuitive. As you come into relationship with your parts, they are encouraged to separate from Self, allowing Self to lead and make decisions that embody the essential qualities of Self: compassion, confidence, clarity, courage, creativity, calm, curiosity, and connectedness. These qualities are often called the eight Cs, and we'll talk more about these qualities and call them into action throughout the book.

The meditations lead you through scenes with the guidance of ancestors to connect with your parts. You are encouraged to get to know parts of yourself, to create space between your parts and Self, and to develop a trusting Self-to-part relationship. The meditation work is supported and expanded with exercises to broaden the experience by further helping parts feel seen, heard, and appreciated.

In Conjunction with Therapy and Coaching

As a consultant to therapists and coaches, I have found that most of them are constantly seeking ways to deepen changes, learning, and healing outside of their sessions. The real work of therapy and coaching takes place in the client's life, so offering homework enables the client to practice in the world what is learned. Most therapists and practitioners see their clients once a week for 60 minutes, and although deep work occurs in these sessions, clients benefit by remaining connected to the work and their parts between sessions. This book offers meditations, exercises, and homework assignments to complete in the in-between time to deepen session work. The book can also be used during a session for guided meditation, working through exercises together in support of the work and to educate clients about the model.

For Therapists and Practitioners

One of the true gifts I've received as an IFS therapist is the healing of doing my own work. Being a healed healer (or at least working toward healing) is a gift we give not only to ourselves, but to our clients. The greater access we have to Self-energy, the more effective we are in our work with clients. This model asserts that Self is the healing agent of the system, ours, and our clients. If we truly believe and subscribe to this assumption, then getting to know our parts and offering healing to them makes sense. This book can help therapists and practitioners do their own personal work to become more healed healers.

I invite you into the world of parts within this book and within yourself. As you read through each chapter, my hope for you is that you develop an intimate relationship with parts of yourself, either for the first time or in a deeper way. By the time you reach the end of this book, I wish you a new level of healing, wholeness, and appreciation for your parts, and ultimately for your Self.

CHAPTER 2

Connecting Inside

Meeting Your Parts

Carefree is the name she had before she became a people pleaser. When Carefree had not a care in the world, she had an easygoing manner that drew children and adults alike into her orbit, and she was only a child herself. She heard adults use words like *full of life, creative, talkative, engaging, a joy to be around* when speaking of her. The words sounded nice to her, and she also knew words didn't and couldn't fully capture her essence. She had an awareness that she was more than the words people used to describe her. She felt light and at home in her body. The world she lived in was exciting, limitless, and full of possibilities. She awoke each day free of worry and fear. She possessed a knowing that she was the creator of her experience, and the options were infinite.

The changes in Carefree didn't happen at once. Life at home, school, and in her neighborhood chipped away at her. She came to learn that being herself was less valuable than being who people wanted her to be. At first, she made little shifts to accommodate the expectations of others.

With each change, no matter how insignificant it seemed at the time, Carefree became less of herself. Worry and fear crept into her existence. The light and comfortable feeling in her body became heavy and foreign. Instead of experiencing life as limitless and full of possibilities, it became finite with right and wrong choices and outcomes. Safety and certainty were no longer found within her but were dependent on her meeting the needs and expectations of others. Her easygoing, fun-loving energy was met with disapproving frowns and statements like "You play too much" or "You need to take this seriously." Once Carefree no longer heard herself described as full of life and a joy to be around, but as dependable, responsible, and the one you can count on, the transformation was complete. Ultimately, Carefree covered who she was to gain the approval of others and to be liked.

Carefree is one of my parts, and I have distinct memories of who she was and how she moved through the world before she became burdened by the expectations of others. Her innate qualities were not nurtured and viewed as valuable. Instead, she got the message that she needed to change, which made her feel not good enough and misunderstood. She started to change and take on qualities that pleased those around her. The more people liked and approved of her, the further removed she was from her original nature.

The burden of pleasing others while denying myself is one that I still struggle with. Although I people please a lot less, I still have the desire to be liked. When I am being myself, the part that wants people to like me wonders, am I doing enough, am I enough, will people like me if I show them who I really am? When I was a child and received praise for being likable, I didn't know any other way to be.

I wasn't seeking approval. I was just being me. The freedom to truly be who I am, with no care about being liked or not, is what I seek.

Who is the "I" speaking in the paragraph you just read? Is it me, or is it Carefree? Is the me that is me separate from the me that is Carefree?

That paragraph is from Carefree's perspective. This is her experience. And we are not separate. She is a part of me. I view my parts and the parts of the people I work with as individual humans with feelings, ideas, beliefs, life experiences. It is important to mention that our parts may or may not appear as we do. For instance, some of our parts share our gender, racial identities, and sexual orientation while other parts do not. You will see later in one of my opening vignettes that I have male-identified parts although I identify as female. Viewing parts as the subpersonalities they are helps me to better relate to my parts and the parts of others. However, when Carefree is in my seat of consciousness, my experience of the world is from her perspective. Carefree is the part of me that still carries some of the people-pleasing burden and desires to return to her unburdened state.

IFS CONCEPT 1: PROTECTIVE NATURE OF PARTS

When we are born, our parts are in their natural state. In most cases, they are not burdened. They can express the full nature of who they are: playful, curious, calm, free, loving, to name a few. However, as children, when our needs for attention, affection, acceptance, and nurturance go unmet, are made fun of, or are denied, our natural ways of being become exiled. We learn that it isn't safe to be fully who we are. We learn that parts of us are unlovable, not good enough, shameful, and should be hidden.

Parts take on roles to protect us from feeling these strong feelings of worthlessness. They do this in one of two ways: They keep us from experiencing the strong feelings by controlling everything they can, keeping us too busy, focused on other things, or distracted to feel our unmet needs. Or, when something in our life triggers our feelings of not-good-enough or shame, parts swoop in to douse the severity of these feelings with intense distractions to take the attention off the emotional pain.

We call both these types of parts "protectors." Some protectors protect in a proactive way to keep us feeling secure and from feeling pain and vulnerability. These are called managers because their role is to manage our lives so as to protect us from pain. These parts make a vow to work relentlessly so we never experience the hurt we felt before they took on the job of protecting us. Carefree exiled her innate nature when she believed it was no longer valued. She searched around her to find what was of value and discovered that those closest to Carefree—her parents, teachers, and relatives—liked her most when she fit their ideal of her. By pleasing others, Carefree did not have to feel the pain of not being good enough. Her true self felt not enough to receive the love and attention from those most important to her. To ensure she didn't have to feel that pain, she became what others needed and expected, and in return she received love and approval. Carefree decided that if she couldn't be accepted and loved for who she was, she would contort herself into someone others couldn't help but love, accept, and approve of.

Here are a few examples of how managers operate. Parts may have learned to protect by being high-achieving, depressed, or perfect. The high-achieving part may believe that the only way to have value is to out-achieve everyone else, and if the person receives praise for the strategies of this part, the part's beliefs and behaviors are rewarded. A part that is depressed may remain in a state of hopelessness to protect the system from feeling something worse, like shame. Another way managers may protect us from feeling inadequate is by pursuing perfection. The perfectionistic part may believe that if it does everything perfectly, we will always feel good enough and we won't have to experience the pain connected to feelings of worthlessness. The parts in these examples use these strategies as an attempt to protect us by managing and controlling the external environment, people, and situations to ensure that the parts of us who have been wounded are not hurt again.

We also have parts that protect in a reactive manner by extinguishing the pain once we are already experiencing it. We call these parts firefighters. The behaviors, beliefs, and strategies they have developed are automatic, and they believe there are no alternatives. These reactive parts use tactics like dissociation, overeating, self-harm, and suicidal thoughts or actions because anything, even if it hurts us in some way, is better than the overwhelming feeling of vulnerability. When vulnerability is expressed, a reactive part may employ dissociation to take us away from feeling exposed. In the part's mind, it is more desirable to be mentally whisked away from a situation than to risk emotional exposure or harm. Another shutdown tactic of reactive firefighter parts is self-harm. When the pain of wounded parts gets triggered, a part who uses self-harm may spring into action. The focus is immediately drawn away from emotional pain to the activity of harming the body. In a more extreme case, parts with suicidal thoughts/actions are protecting us too. Although this sounds counterintuitive, these parts remind us that if the pain becomes unbearable, we have a way out. The irony of parts with suicidal behaviors is they do not want us to die. They want the pain of living to cease and have no idea how to make that happen other than to kill us.

IFS CONCEPT 2: GO INSIDE (FIND, FOCUS, FEEL TOWARD)

The overall goal of IFS therapy is to release parts from the roles they were forced into to protect us. We accomplish this by first noticing their presence. We notice by going inside. Our parts exist inside of us and sometimes slightly outside of us. To notice them, we need to move our attention from the external world to our internal one. We can do this by quietly closing our eyes, softening our gaze, or looking downward. Upon entering our internal world, we pause to notice who is present. Parts may present themselves as sensations, emotions, images, words, thoughts, memories, an inner voice, physical symptoms, or a felt sense. Once we turn our awareness inside, we may notice a sensation like tingling in the stomach. We want to pause and focus on that sensation. As we focus, we want to see what else is present. Often when we bring our attention to a part, it may expand, express other sides of itself, or remain the same. We might even experience another part expressing itself too. Whatever comes up is okay. We are simply noticing and focusing. Next, we want to ask, "How do I feel toward what I'm noticing?" We may feel uneasy, scared, calm, curious—a number of different feelings can surface. I will share more about this process in later chapters, but these are the beginning steps of going inside and noticing our parts.

Case Vignette: Raging Firefighter

The client, Romero, is a late-40s biracial male with a Black father and a white mother. He is gay, married to a Latino male for 12 years, and they have no children. Romero sought therapy because his partner threatened to end the marriage if he didn't get help for his anger. Romero was sexually abused from ages 8 to 11 by a male family friend, and he admits that he carries a lot of anger about having his childhood "stolen in that way." He and I started his IFS work with the part that was angry about being sexually abused.

It became clear early on that this part was not only angry about the sexual abuse but blamed Romero for what happened to him. The anger, rage, and disdain of this part became apparent in a session where Romero started to express sadness by crying about what happened to his younger self.

"What the fuck are you crying for?" the part barked and glared. I had an awareness that the tender feelings Romero was expressing toward his younger self had been usurped by another part. The new part in the driver's seat seemed to hold contempt for the tears. I asked the part, "Who are you?" and he answered, "I'm Byron, who the fuck are you?" I let Byron know that I was Romero's therapist and that I was here to help Romero.

"Good luck, his punk-ass can't be helped," Byron spat. I got the sense that Byron didn't like Romero, and I asked him why he spoke so harshly toward him.

"Damn, do you really need to ask? Just look at him. Weak, good for nothing."

"Tell me more about how you came to view him this way."

With a mean mug scowl, Byron said, "Only a punk would let a man rape him."

"So, you believe it was Romero's fault that his abuser hurt him."

"Of course. He's weak and didn't stand up for himself. Like now, he's crying and snotting about things he can't change. He needs to man up."

"Let me get this straight: You stepped in because Romero was crying and feeling the pain of what happened to him?"

"Right, he doesn't need to feel that shit, and if he does, I shut it the fuck down."

"Is your job to keep Romero from feeling pain?"

"His punk-ass couldn't handle it if I didn't."

Byron is true to his job as a firefighter. When Romero started experiencing the pain of his younger self who was abused, Byron turned the hose on full blast to extinguish Romero's emotions. Initially, Byron would only talk to me. It took several months of sessions of Byron being in relationship with me before he was willing to consider being in relationship with Romero. Even when Byron warmed to the idea of him and Romero getting to know each other, he was skeptical: "I'll try this shit, but nothing's going to change."

The other challenge within Romero's system was the existence of parts who were afraid of Byron. Even when Byron consented to getting to know Romero, there were parts who were fearful of Romero's safety if he got close to Byron. They believed Romero couldn't handle Byron's fury and disdain. Parts within our systems respond to firefighters the same way people in the world do. When firefighters express their rage in the world, some people respond by cowering and fearing them. The same thing happens internally. Once we worked with the parts that feared a relationship between Romero and Byron, we were able to shift our work to establishing a relationship between the two with my support.

Romero entered the conversation with Byron with compassion and curiosity. He had a true desire to understand Byron's harshness toward him. Being in the presence of curiosity instead of judgment or fear was a new experience for Byron. It helped him to decrease his intensity. Byron was encouraged to tell Romero about himself. "I have to be mean to toughen you up," he said.

Romero asked, "Where did you learn to be so mean?"

Byron paused thoughtfully and answered, "I learned from what happened to you. You need to be hard, strong, so no one will hurt you like that again. It's my job to make you tough." With this new information and clarity, I suggested that Romero ask Byron if he was aware that he was using demeaning and humiliating tactics like those of his abuser. Upon realizing he had become Romero's internalized abuser, Byron lowered his head and voice and tearfully said, "No, I didn't know that."

IFS CONCEPT 3: FIREFIGHTERS INTENT VS. IMPACT

The intention of our firefighters is to protect us from pain and vulnerability. They are highly reactive to the experience or near experience of feelings that they view as harmful to us. They employ behaviors that are unacceptable in society and to parts within our internal systems. Firefighters get the message that what they do (rage, self-harm, use drugs, gamble, cheat on their partner, etc.) is objectionable. Managers within the system try to control and shut down their behavior, and people and systems in society attempt to shut them down too. However, they cannot cease their behavior until what they protect is healed.

Due to their ferocity in protecting, they are unaware of their negative impact. Firefighters impact on multiple levels. Often there are parts within the system that are fearful of the firefighters, like the parts within Romero that were afraid he would be further harmed by being in relationship with Byron. This is also true of people in our lives who have to relate to our reactive parts. We saw in the vignette that Romero's partner had reached the point of possible divorce if he did not address his anger. We also saw that Byron had no idea of how his behavior was similar in nature to Romero's abuser. Byron's intention was not to abuse Romero further, but to make him strong so he could protect himself from abuse.

In the same way Romero got to know his part Byron who carried the anger of his abuse, you can begin to get to know your parts. One of the reasons for coming into a relationship with your parts is to understand their positive intentions, not just their impact. Remember one of the assumptions of IFS is that all parts are well-intentioned, regardless of how they express themselves. I invite you to use the meditation and exercises in this chapter to begin to get to know at least one of your parts. You may want to start with one of your managers, as firefighters can be more challenging. If you would like to listen to the meditation, a recording is available for you to download. You can find instructions for accessing the recording in the opening pages of the book. So, pull out your journal and begin the exploration of your internal family system.

Meditation: Connecting Inside

Awareness of our parts and the ability to connect and build relationships with them is foundational to the healing process. As I explained in the introduction, most of the meditations in this book were co-created with the ancestors of my mother's mother's line.

This meditation helps you go inside, notice part(s), and learn a little about them by connecting.

Bring your attention to your breath.

Notice how your breath moves in and out of your body.

Move your attention from your external world to your internal world by closing your eyes or softening your gaze, or whatever feels comfortable for you.

As you go inside, see if you can notice the presence of a part.

Whatever is present is okay. Be with whatever shows itself.

Now take a closer look. What more do you notice about the part?

> Is there a color?
>
> Do you notice a bodily sensation?
>
> What does it say, if anything?
>
> Ask the part its name.

Let the part know you're there while allowing it to be however it needs to be.

Take note of what else it shows or shares with you.

Are you curious to know more about this part?

If so, you might ask, "What do you want me to know about you?"

Listen with openness and curiosity.

Encourage the part to share as much of its experience as it would like.

When that feels complete, ask the part what it needs from you.

After you learn what the part needs, see if there's anything else it wants to share.

Set an intention to come back and connect with the part again.

If it feels right, express appreciation.

Slowly bring your awareness back to your breath.

Open your eyes when you're ready.

Exercise 1: Journal Capture

Take out your journal and quickly write whatever you would like to capture from this meditation. It could be a revelation, a reflection, a fleeting thought, or sensory perception.

Exercise 2: Connecting Inside Journal Questions

After you've done the Connecting Inside meditation and written your quick Journal Capture, take some time to explore more deeply by responding to the following journal prompts.

1. How are you feeling after connecting with your part?
2. If you were not able to connect with a part, what happened inside?
3. What did you learn about your part?
4. If your part expressed itself as a bodily sensation, describe where and what you experienced?
5. How does this part show up in your life?
6. How will you honor what the part needs from you?
7. What intentions did you set with your part?

Exercise 3: Connecting Inside

Take a moment to go inside and connect with your part again. Notice how you experience the part, then ask the part how it would like you to draw or represent it in the box below or in your journal. The level of artistry is unimportant. Parts may want to be drawn simply, as a zigzag line or a circle, or with greater detail. When you are clear about how it wants to be represented, draw the part.

After drawing the picture, answer the questions below.

1. What more do you notice about the part?
2. As you look at the picture, ask the part, "Is there anything else you want me to know about you?"
3. How can you remain in connection with this part of yourself?

CHAPTER 3

The Meadow

Young and Vulnerable Parts

Raised voices scare me. I don't know what will happen next. Something bad usually happens after the shouting. Don't they know their voices make me shake inside? When I shake, I cry. Hi, I'm five and they call me Cry Baby. I don't think that's my real name, but it's the one everyone calls me. I didn't think crying was bad or good. I just cry when I need to. But most of the big people tell me, "Don't cry. Be a big girl." I hear that a lot. Crying must be bad. Why else would they tell me not to do it? It's confusing because crying makes me feel better. So, if I feel like I'm going to cry, I try hard to hold it in. If I can't hold it in, I cry alone in my room, the bathroom, outside, anywhere no one will see me crying. I wonder if something is wrong with me. Maybe that's why I cry so much. I wish they could feel what it's like inside of me. I have big, big feelings. Some of them are bigger than me. When I feel happy, I get silly and giggly. When I feel sad or scared, I hide and cry. When I feel mad, my body gets hot, and I yell. I think happy is good because the big people like it when I'm happy.

I don't think they know, but I feel their feelings too. I'm a sponge for feelings. Sometimes I wonder if the feelings are mine or not mine. It gets hard to tell. They get jumbly inside. Somehow, I know when other people are happy, mad, sad, or scared without them telling me. I feel it in my body. I think sometimes my tears aren't mine but theirs.

Oh no, I hear my mother shouting for me, "Tamala! Come here! Get in here right now!" I run as fast as I can and find her in the den of my grandmother's house. Her tone of voice scares me. I try to hold back the tears, but I can't. My mother yells, "What are you crying for?" This makes me cry harder. "Tamala, I only called you in here. This crying doesn't make any sense. Stop it! Stop it now!" My grandmother adds, "Stop all that crying. Nothing's wrong. You can't be *that* sensitive!" Hearing how my mother and grandmother respond to my tears convinces me that crying and being sensitive is bad. I decide I will work harder to not cry and be less sensitive, whatever that means.

IFS CONCEPT 1: EXILES

Exiles are usually young, vulnerable parts of us that hide from awareness for self-protection or that protectors attempt to keep hidden for fear they will destabilize the system with their pain and vulnerability. When we are young and unburdened, these parts may express as joyous, curious, playful, and energetic. However, they receive the message from family, cultural groups, and society that their natural way of being is unacceptable. Children come to understand that who they are is not okay, and to receive love and care, they need to change who and how they are. This creates the need to exile or cut off parts of themselves from the whole. Children are vulnerable and dependent on adults, and if rejecting parts of themselves is the cost of their safety, love, and care, the system adjusts to increase the likelihood the child will receive the care needed to survive. The system will keep adjusting to outside forces, exiling more parts if necessary.

Exiling is the result of trauma, attachment injuries, and devaluing experiences. Traumatic events experienced in childhood include physical and emotional abuse, sexual abuse, physical and emotional neglect, abandonment, accidents, and injury. Attachment injuries occur when childhood caregivers are unable or unwilling to meet the child's needs for care, comfort, affection, and attention. This can range from lack of attunement to complete disregard of needs. Devaluing experiences include bullying, shaming, name-calling, disdainful looks, criticism, and rejection. Experiencing any one of these events or in combination in response to being your natural self as a child communicates the message that something is wrong with you. Children are motivated to fit the norms of family, school, culture, and community; therefore, parts are exiled to conform.

IFS CONCEPT 2: BURDENS

Burdens are extreme emotions, beliefs, and energies absorbed by parts because of trauma, attachment injury, and devaluing experiences. Burdens are created through personal interactions, cultural experiences, and generational transmission. Personal burdens are based on our firsthand or lived experiences. The natural state of my part that I shared at the beginning of this chapter was sensitivity to her own feelings/emotions and those of others. She felt deeply and was comfortable with expressing her feelings. However, she received messages from her family that her sensitivity was too much, it wasn't okay to cry, and when she did, she was being a "cry baby." The burden that this part acquired was the belief that she was too much, being sensitive and crying was bad, and she needed to hide those aspects of herself to be accepted and loved. Anytime she felt tearful emotion rising within, she would stifle it, and if she couldn't stop it, she would apologize for the tears.

Cultural burdens are those we absorb from the dominant culture. The four cultural burdens of the United States identified by Schwartz and Sweezy are racism, patriarchy, materialism, and individualism.[1] There are also burdens passed down through family and ancestral lines that are not a part of the person's lived experience; these are called legacy burdens. We'll discuss cultural and legacy burdens more fully in Chapter 11. It is possible for burdens to be 100 percent personal; some combination of the types, such as part personal and part legacy; or a blend of all three types.

IFS CONCEPT 3: WITNESSING

More than anything, exiles seek redemption and desire to tell their story. In their quest for redemption, they seek love and validation from the person who harmed them or someone who has qualities like that person. They are highly motivated to tell their story, which often causes them to behave in a needy manner. Faulty thinking causes them to believe that by letting others know what happened to them and being redeemed, they will feel validated, loved, and worthy. Our exiles cause us to lead with our trauma histories to bond with others. Exiles are often searching for the care they did not receive as children. Since Self is the healing energy in our system, it is being in relationship and sharing their stories with Self that results in exiles truly experiencing the love, care, and validation they seek.

Witnessing is the beginning of the healing process for exiles. This is an exchange where exiles get to tell their story in the presence of a compassionate, curious, calm, and connected listener and witness. When exiles are engaged with any of the eight qualities of Self-energy, the process of reparenting begins. (I'll talk more about these qualities in Chapter 4.) The exiles get to experience an adult being there for them in a way they may never have experienced in the past. Asking exiles what they want to share about their experiences, with genuine interest, encourages them to share their pains in words, bodily sensations, emotions, movement, images, and any other way that helps them to be understood by Self. It is important for Self to respond to what the exile is sharing to deepen trust and connection between the two of them. Asking if there's more helps the exile share their story fully. No matter what or how the exile shares, Self can handle it and support them to tell their story until they feel heard and understood. The witnessing process is complete when the exile has nothing more to share and feels fully understood by Self.

Case Vignette: An Exile's Story

Kirsten is a 28-year-old Caucasian female who sought therapy for unresolved childhood trauma. She is recently engaged and concerned that if she doesn't address her history, it will negatively impact her marriage. She grew up with married parents and two siblings significantly older than her. By the time she was eight, both siblings were away at college. She describes her parents as "unhappily married," saying her father had multiple affairs and her mother endured his "emotional and physical abuse." Kirsten felt like an unwanted obligation for her father and a possession to her mother instead of a desired and loved child. After working with several of Kirsten's protectors, we received permission to connect with an exile named Unwanted.

Kirsten felt sincere and immense compassion for Unwanted and shared her desire to get to know Unwanted's story. This exile was slow to warm up to Kirsten because no one had shown genuine interest in her before. I instructed Kirsten to extend her compassionate energy to Unwanted until she noticed any shift in Unwanted. Kirsten was silent for a while, then said, "She has moved closer to me." The closeness deepened Kirsten's compassion and curiosity toward Unwanted. With the strengthened connection, I asked Kirsten if she was interested in learning Unwanted's story. She was very interested and let Unwanted know.

Unwanted chose to tell her story in multiple scenes from her life, played like a movie. Kirsten shared what she was viewing with me, as I'll share it with you now.

The first scene is of Unwanted at the dinner table with her parents. She notices her mother seems nervous and on edge as Dad starts to eat. He yells and complains that the food is horrible, shouting, "It's a shame my girlfriend cooks better than my wife. Maybe you should take cooking lessons from her." He throws his plate against the wall, causing Unwanted to jump in fear. Her dad threatens to leave. Her mother begs him to stay. Unwanted is scared for him to go *or* stay. When her father gets up from the table and starts walking to the door, her mother chases after him, crying, and tries to block the door. He yanks her away from the door, pointing at the mess he made, demanding she clean it up, then storms out and slams the door. Kirsten reports that this is a regular occurrence in her home. Dad either doesn't come home from work; comes home, eats dinner, and leaves; or complains about what is prepared, gets angry, and leaves.

The next scene shared by Unwanted causes Kirsten's body to shake and tremble. She is shown multiple images of her mother taking care of her in ways and at times in which she could care for herself but was not allowed. One scene is of her mother insisting on bathing her when she was 10 years old, another of her mother cutting her food and feeding it to her around the same age, and another at age 8 of her mother coming in the bathroom to help her wipe herself, saying, "I want to make sure you're clean." Unwanted shares, "If I insisted I could do things myself, my mother would cry and accuse me of being selfish and not loving her."

Kirsten asks if there's more. Unwanted continues that she felt helpless and had a hard time separating herself from her mother. At times, she felt like her body wasn't her own but belonged to her mother.

Unwanted describes the final scene as loud, scary, dark, and violent. She speaks directly to me instead of to Kirsten. "It started at the dinner table with my mother threatening to divorce my father if he didn't stop cheating. My father lost it. He broke dishes, lamps, ripped pictures off the wall. He was out of control. My mother grabbed me and yelled for him to stop. That only fueled his rage, and he grabbed her, causing me to fall to the floor. I quickly crawled under the dining room table. I heard him punch her repeatedly. Her screaming made it hard for me to breathe. We were all screaming. My mother fell to the floor with my father on top of her. I saw him choking her. Her dead and desperate eyes connected with my terrified ones. Her face was bloodied. I screamed for him to stop. I was afraid he would kill her. My screaming finally got his attention. He looked down at his hands around my mother's neck as if he was shocked to find them there. He looked back at me and then back at his hands. He released my mother and ran out of the house. I crawled into the arms of my coughing and crying mother, unsure who was comforting who."

I ask Kirsten to ask Unwanted if there is anything else she wants to share. Unwanted shares that she saw her mother get beaten many times, but this was the worst and scariest because she thought her mother was going to die. I ask Kirsten to check and see if Unwanted feels understood and heard by her. Kirsten nods and tells me what Unwanted has said: "Finally, someone understands what happened to me."

The entire time Kirsten was sharing the last scene, she and Unwanted were both in the seat of consciousness. Sometimes the client will witness the exile's story by being with the part, and other times the client will be the part. When the client is the part, the exile is speaking directly to the therapist, sharing its story and connecting with the therapist. This back and forth between being with and being the part can occur multiple times within the witnessing of one memory. I find this endearing when it happens because it feels like the part is trusting me as the therapist and wants to share their story more intimately with me.

Meditation: The Meadow

The Meadow meditation is the third given to me by my ancestors. While doing my own IFS therapy and working with my exiles, my ancestors allowed me to connect more fully with one of my exiles through this meditation.

This meditation allows you to meet and get to know a new exile or deepen a connection with one you've met before.

Close your eyes or soften your gaze.

Adjust your body until it settles.

Bring your awareness to your breath and just breathe.

As you go inside, notice the pause at the end of each inhale and exhale. Right before the next inhale or exhale, there's a space. Pause at that space.

Follow your breath through your body several times, noticing the pause.

Find yourself in a sunlit meadow with all the scents of spring in the air.

The tall grass waves in the wind.

The sun is warm on your face.

And you notice a cool breeze.

Walking in the warmth, you see a small child sitting on a patch of grass with their back to you.

As you walk closer, you recognize the child as a younger you.

You sense the child's emotions and get as close as the child will allow.

What do you notice about the younger you?

How do you feel toward them?

If those feelings are open and/or positive, send the energy of those feelings to your younger self.

If the feelings are not warm or positive, see if the parts with those feelings will step back and allow you to be with your younger self. If they will not step back, explore their concerns and/or fears.

As you send your younger self the positive energy, see if they will allow you to come closer.

Be with your younger self in whatever way they need you to be there.

If they want to talk, listen.

If they want to be held, hold them.

If they want to play, play with them, or watch them play.

Whatever they need, be there for them.

Ask your younger self if there's more they need from you.

Continue your time in the meadow together in whatever way your younger self needs.

Now that you're connected, let your younger self know they always have you.

See if there's anything more either of you want to share with the other before it's time to go.

See if there's a place your younger self would like to stay until the two of you connect again. If so, take your younger self to that place.

Let your younger self know it is time for you to leave, and reassure them that you will connect with them again.

Bring your awareness to your breath and the space between each inhale and exhale. When you're ready, re-enter this moment and space by slowly opening your eyes.

Exercise 1: Journal Capture

Take out your journal and quickly write whatever you would like to capture from this meditation. It could be a revelation, a reflection, a fleeting thought, or sensory perception.

Exercise 2: The Meadow Journal Questions

After you've done the Meadow meditation and written your quick Journal Capture, take some time to explore more deeply by responding to the following journal prompts.

1. What are the first things you noticed about your younger self?

2. What emotions did you sense from the younger you when you first came upon them?
3. Were you already familiar with this part of yourself? If so, how has this part expressed itself in the past?
4. How did you feel toward the part? If it was positive or warm, how did the part respond?
5. If it was not positive or warm, what parts came up and what were their fears or concerns?
6. What did your younger self need from you?
7. What is the significance of this part showing up today?

Exercise 3: Deepen the Connection

Connect with this part daily for a week to learn more about them.

Ask the part what more it wants to share with you.

Ask the part what has been difficult for it.

What did it need that it didn't get?

Journal what you learn.

CHAPTER 4

Self Qualities

The You That's Not a Part

I sit in a translucent golden bubble. I am safe. I am present. I am open. I not only hear their words, but I feel them. I am leading an IFS training where some participants expected an affinity space for BIPOC (Black, Indigenous, People of Color) attendees, while others anticipated an affinity space for Black folks only. However, the training is designed to include predominantly people who identify as Black, followed by a smaller number of people who identify as BIPOC, and then a lesser number of participants who identify as white. Because most of the attendees did not expect the training to include white people, their parts feel unsafe, disappointed, fearful, angry, defensive, and harmed.

IFS training sessions are designed to use the model to address any conflict or difficulties that arise in the training. Therefore, processing time is built into the design of the training. However, this training required more processing than any other that I have led because so many people were activated so intensely. Every day of the training required some amount of processing related to the racial and ethnic makeup of the training cohort. As the lead trainer and the most visible, I was the target of the participants' anger, rage, and blame. I realized from this experience there are situations that no amount of training and mentoring can prepare you for. What *did* prepare me to remain in my seat, without my parts taking over, was my commitment to my own IFS therapy that I had been doing for five years before this training.

In the most heated exchange and processing, I heard the following accusations from participants: "Leadership tricked us. We were led to believe this was going to be a safe place; I don't feel safe. I didn't expect to see white people in a training for BIPOC folks. Leadership has heard our complaints and hasn't done anything to fix the problem. It doesn't seem like leadership cares. We are being harmed in this training, and leadership isn't doing anything about it." Over and over, I heard, "I don't feel safe, I'm being harmed, leadership doesn't care enough to do anything to take care of me, and my needs are not important."

Prior to learning about my system of parts and being in relationship with them, I would have become defensive and frustrated, justifying why things were the way they were, and attempting to explain my way out of a difficult situation. Instead, my parts did not take over. They trusted me. As I sat in my golden bubble, I envisioned each blaming statement as a fiery arrow leaving the hand of the one talking being shot toward me. As each flaming arrow got closer, it transformed into the pain under their words of blame and finger pointing. I saw the depth of their hurt, disappointment, fear, lack of safety, and unworthiness of their needs being met. I did not experience their words as a personal attack as I would have in my past. I experienced their words as requests for what they needed and I met them with compassion, calm, and curiosity. I genuinely wanted to understand what the participants were feeling and experiencing.

I also wanted to help ease their pain. Therefore, I not only listened, but I also encouraged them to tell me more. I didn't shy away from the conversation I would have found quite difficult in the past. I delved deeper to understand more fully. I didn't only listen with compassion and curiosity; I extended my Self-energy toward them. I let them experience that I could hold whatever the truth of their feelings was. To help them to trust me more, I took complete responsibility for what had happened—for the lack of clarity about the racial composition of the training. I expressed my understanding of how shocking and disappointing this must be for them. I assumed nothing. I asked them to share with me the injuries they experienced and what they needed from me as a repair. I persisted in my commitment to help them feel seen, heard, and understood by me.

This experience taught me that Self-energy can hold big emotions. It can hold the pain of others. It can be the connection between the expression of hurt and the relief of that hurt with understanding. I learned that I am not harmed by the expression of someone else's pain, even when that expression is directed at me. I also had an awareness that I was not efforting or searching for the "right" words to say. I wasn't trying to placate, people-please or caretake the participants. Accessing my Self qualities allowed me to be with what was present in the room with the confidence of a compassionate listener connecting with the pain of those sharing. I remained curious to know their experiences as fully as they were willing to share. I had the courage to ask for clarity to deepen my understanding, and keeping a calm head made space for creative offerings to improve the situation. Through the entire process, the confidence of Self maintained that I could handle their concerns, repair the unintended impact, and not be diminished by their upset.

IFS CONCEPT 1: SELF QUALITIES

Self is universal, and everyone has access to Self. It is who we are when we are not blended with one of our extreme parts. Self is whole and unaffected by the hurts and traumas we have experienced. This is the deepest essence or center of every person. Self is wise, intuitive, and able to heal and lead. The only agenda held by Self is one of healing detached from controlling how and when healing takes place. Self never goes away. However, we may lose connection to Self because of the harshness, abuses, and attachment injuries we've experienced. An analogy to describe what happens when we have little or no access to Self is the same as when clouds obscure the sun on an overcast day. The sun does not go away. It is still present but covered by the clouds. No matter how dampened or covered up Self may become, it is still present. The key is to bring awareness to our parts and develop a relationship between Self and our parts.

Self has eight essential qualities, as we saw in Chapter 1—the eight Cs. When Self is expressed, we experience one or more of these qualities. The qualities are compassion, curiosity, calm, connectedness, confidence, clarity, creativity, and courage. The qualities are defined by Dr. Richard Schwartz[1] and Julia Sullivan,[2] a Level 2–trained IFS therapist, as follows:

Compassion: The ability to see suffering and feel for another. It is different from empathy, which is feeling *with* another. When we have compassion for others, we want to do something to relieve their suffering. We simultaneously have empathy for the other and a belief that the other has a Self that can relieve the other's own suffering. Compassion allows us to see beyond others' angry parts to the fear or pain behind them. We can apply these concepts of compassion to our own parts as well in the form of self-compassion. Self offers compassion to our parts when they are attempting to deal with challenging life situations. Parts need to know through the experience of Self that they are not alone and have a resource to support and guide them.

Curiosity: The ability to have a sense of wonder about the world and how things work. The ability to ask questions without an agenda. A genuine interest in knowing another's perspective. It is the ability to bring agenda-free curiosity to your own actions too. The ability to show genuine interest in why people behave as they do or why they feel the way they do instead of becoming upset about what they say or do. Self allows natural curiosity when faced with another person's anger or upset. Curiosity replaces our defensiveness or upset.

Calm: The ability to experience physiological and mental serenity regardless of the circumstances. The ability to reduce activity of the mind and body. We remain physically calm during stressful situations, and we can have a peaceful presence with other people and with our parts. The Self quality of calm allows us to be with another's upset without becoming defensive.

Connectedness: The ability to maintain connection with others and to every part of ourself. A desire to reconnect when disconnection occurs. It is feeling a part of a larger entity or community. When in connection with another, we feel accepted and can relax our defenses because we know we won't be judged, controlled, or hurt. There's also a knowing that any misunderstandings can be repaired because of the connection. The quality of connectedness allows us to remain in relationship with our parts even when they do things we do not like or are not proud of, recognizing that all of life is connected and the sense of separateness is an illusion.

Confidence: A strong belief in one's ability to handle or repair whatever happens in life. The ability to be self-assured and know that we are worthwhile and valuable even when we make mistakes or others are upset with us. Confidence allows us not to be reduced or made to feel less-than by someone else's negative evaluations of us or by their being upset with us.

Clarity: The ability to maintain a clear, undistorted view of situations without extreme beliefs or emotions. The ability to have a "beginner's mind" in which many possibilities exist. Clarity affords us the opportunity to take in the necessary information to make the best decision.

Creativity: The ability to explore and enjoy novelty. The ability to enter the "flow state" in which expression spontaneously flows out of us while we're engaged in a pleasurable activity. The ability to encourage our parts to express themselves without shame, fear, or worthlessness. Creativity produces out-of-the-box thinking. The Self quality of creativity leads us to new and novel solutions to problems.

Courage: The strength to face threat, challenge, or danger. The ability to recognize, apologize, and make amends for any damage caused by our words or actions. The willingness to reflect and "go inside" toward our own pain and shame, come into relationship with hurting parts, and heal the pain. The ability to speak for our extreme parts like anger, disappointment, criticism in a way that does not hurt others. The willingness to speak up for injustice. The Self quality of courage allows us to engage in ways and do things that parts of us are afraid to do.

Everyone has a Self; however, our access to it may be limited by our parts. Access to Self is granted by the parts when they choose to relax and step back. When parts do this, Self can lead the internal family of parts through the expression of the eight qualities. It is the resource that heals the trauma and pain of the past.

IFS CONCEPT 2: SELF-LIKE PARTS

There are parts in the system that can appear like the Self but are not the Self. These parts are referred to as Self-like parts. They are managers who keep the system in balance by behaving similarly and possessing qualities like the Self. They are empathetic, care, and want to help, but they cannot heal parts—only Self can do that. Because Self-like parts respond from empathy, not compassion, they act from a desire to protect other parts, especially exiled parts, while Self is compassionate toward our parts with an offering of healing. Self is not afraid or overwhelmed by the experiences or wounds held by our vulnerable parts, while Self-like parts will attempt to comfort our wounded parts or keep them hidden, which is a form of protecting them. They may also try to explain away the pain of what happened to us when we were young.

You may notice your Self-like parts when interacting with others or in relationship with other parts. To identify one, notice if your heart is open or closed. Ask yourself, does the part seem to have an agenda? Although Self wants to help our parts heal, it doesn't push for healing. It offers healing as a choice and allows parts to decide. Self-like parts, on the other hand, try to push parts—and other people—in a particular direction. When Self-like parts express curiosity, it is often a figure-it-out type of curiosity coming from the head, while the curiosity of Self comes from a true desire to know about the other without any agenda.

Ancestors and Access to Self

Our ancestors hold great knowledge about our lineage, history, strengths, and challenges. Connecting with them and their wisdom can enhance the healing process. Bringing your ancestors into the process creates greater access to Self, both your own and your ancestors'. As we saw earlier, Self is the healing agent within our system. Therefore, it makes sense that having more access to Self internally and externally can positively impact the healing process.

Connecting with your ancestors in the IFS healing process increases the amount of Self-energy available for healing. Instead of only having access to your Self-energy (which is sufficient for healing all by itself), you magnify the amount and intensity of Self-energy by inviting connection with your Self-led ancestors. This increase of Self-energy may help you to heal more quickly, more deeply, and more completely. Our ancestors are rooting for us and will assist and support us when we invite them to do so. Just as my ancestors joined me in creating the meditations I share in this book, your ancestors are available as guides in your life too.

Case Vignette: Grieved Empty Nester

Christina, a married 48-year-old Black woman, came to therapy feeling depressed, directionless, useless, and without purpose after her only living son, Evan, graduated from medical school, moved across the country for employment, and asked his girlfriend to marry him. The feelings of loss were compounded by the loss of Evan's identical twin, Kevin, who had died in a boating accident at age 12. Christina realized that she had not allowed herself to fully grieve the earlier loss because she poured herself into her surviving son. Both her sons were on the capsizing boat that took Kevin's life, and she is thankful she did not lose them both.

Prior to Kevin's death, Christina had a vibrant social life. She belonged to local clubs. She spent time traveling with her family and with girlfriends. She was active in her church. She worked in her husband's medical practice as the office manager. However, after the loss of Kevin, she collapsed her life to solely focusing on Evan. He became the center of her world. She pulled back from social engagements. She quit her job. The one connection she maintained outside of her family was to the church. She explained it was the one connection that "kept me from losing my mind."

Our work together was long and arduous. Christina's system was highly protective and did not want to address the connection between Evan's launch into adult life and the earlier loss of his twin, Kevin. She felt comfortable talking about being an empty nester and her desire to find purpose, yet she was unwilling to accept that her son did not need her in the same capacity he once did. She found his behavior toward her dismissive and hurtful. She was jealous of the amount of time he spent with his fiancée and resented how little time he had for her and his father. I noticed an overinvestment in her son's life and little focus on her own, even though she had come into therapy with the stated goal of finding purpose in her life for that very reason: so she wouldn't be hyper-focused on and enmeshed with her son. I realized that to help her create purpose in her life as an empty nester, we would have to come into relationship with the parts of her that were experiencing grief, which she called depression.

Christina made many attempts to re-engage life by resuming activities she had found fulfilling before Kevin's death. She tried crocheting, which had been an enjoyable stress reliever in the past. This time, though, she would start projects, lose interest, and not finish them. Then she would take on a new project with renewed excitement, but within a few weeks she'd discard the new project too. She would make promises to her friends to get together, then cancel as the date approached, sometimes even on the day of the event. She even considered going back to work in her husband's practice or returning to school for an advanced degree, but found reasons not to follow through on either. Her life remained reduced to housekeeping and church.

After Christina and I had spent about a year working with the parts of her that wanted her to find purpose and the parts that blocked or undermined her attempts, one day she arrived at my office bawling uncontrollably. She shared her awareness that she could never have a full life again until she came to terms with the loss of Kevin. This was the first time she had overtly acknowledged a connection between her son's death and her lack of purpose, not to mention expressing willingness to work with the loss.

What we discovered with Christina's system was an alliance of parts working together to keep the pain of her son's death out of her awareness. Some parts did this by keeping her focused on various ways to engage in life, while others undermined this engagement; some held the feelings of sadness, depression, and anger; others kept her hyper-focused on Evan's life and the pain of her decreased involvement in it. In the year we worked together, the parts that wanted to keep the grief out of awareness had gradually learned to trust Christina, me, and the IFS process. After the day she came to session bawling with her newfound awareness, the path and pace of her treatment moved steadily forward. Christina now wanted to face her grief. She saw it as the key to her healing and to discovering new purpose.

Here are some examples of how Christina came into relationship with her parts, using the qualities of Self to get to know each of them.

Christina had several protectors who were grieving the loss of Kevin and managed their grief by keeping busy in various ways. She first came into a relationship with a part who presented her with options to keep busy, such as crocheting, connecting with friends, and going back to school or work. She was genuinely curious about the role of this part in her system. As she showed this part agenda-free curiosity, the part shared that it had to keep busy and distracted to keep from breaking down and to keep Christina safe from a pain so deep that she couldn't possibly survive it. Christina appreciated this part's care and protection; she expressed her compassion for how hard the part had been working and her appreciation of its efforts to keep her from deeper pain.

Next, we met a part carrying anger about the untimely death of Kevin. This part blamed everyone involved. It was critical and blamed Christina for letting the boys go boating that day without either parent present. It blamed the rescue crew for how long it took to pull Kevin out of the water. It blamed the EMTs for not getting him to the hospital fast enough. It blamed the hospital staff. Anyone who had encountered Kevin, directly or indirectly, was culpable and complicit in his death in the eyes of this part. There were other parts in Christina's system that were afraid of this part's fury, but she displayed courage in meeting the level of this part's anger with a greater measure of calm. She also listened to the part's sense of injustice at Kevin's life being taken at such a young age. This part ultimately felt the connection between itself and Christina's Self, and it felt seen and understood.

As we met and got to know more of Christina's protectors, she made another connection: the connection between the loss of Kevin, the launching of Evan, and the death of her mother when Christina was 11. The part that her protectors most wanted to keep out of Christina's awareness was the 11-year-old who hid her unbearable pain away to function in life.

It was only through working with Christina's fiercest protectors, the ones who managed her life through getting her haphazardly involved in new projects and activities, the one hyper-focused on Evan, and the one that held anger and rage, that we found the core trauma that connected it all: the loss of her mother. This pivotal loss was the blueprint for how Christina's system organized itself around future losses. Her ability to engage her parts with the qualities of Self was the catalyst for the deeper healing that came later.

Christina's work befriending her parts and building relationships with them relaxed her protectors enough to reveal this younger part of her who carried the pain of her mother dying. It was working with this younger part, called an exile, that Christina was able to achieve deep healing, to redefine her relationship with Evan, fully grieve Kevin, and re-engage her life.

Meditation: Self Qualities

Note: the majority of the meditations in this book were created with the guidance of my ancestors. I created this meditation and two others without ancestral input. The Self Qualities meditation uses affirmation and intentions to help you connect with the eight qualities of Self. Notice what happens in your system as each statement is heard. Some parts may not agree with the statements or may have a hard time with them. If this happens, notice what the parts are experiencing and make no attempt to change it.

Close your eyes or soften your gaze.
Take note of your breath.
As you breathe, allow your awareness to take notice of each breath.
Notice any shifts as you breathe.
Bring your attention to your breath as it enters your heart space.
Focus on what you're experiencing in your heart.
Do you notice warmth, tightness, a softening, tenderness? Is your heart space open or closed?

Be with what is present as you meditate on the intentions that follow. You may have parts that don't agree or find these statements challenging. If this happens, just be with the parts to understand their concerns.

I have compassion for myself that radiates out to others.

My creativity allows for free expression.

I view situations and people with clarity.

Calmness is the baseline from which I operate.

I maintain connection with every part of myself.

I walk in the wonder of curiosity.

I have the courage to admit and accept when I am wrong.

I have the confidence of knowing I am a worthwhile person no matter what is happening in my world.

I am Confident that there are Creative ways to Connect inside to witness my parts with Clarity, while remaining Calm and being Courageous enough to stay Curious when my parts get activated, remembering that a little Compassion goes a long way.

Bring your awareness to your breath, and if it feels right, just breathe as you re-enter this moment and space.

Slowly open your eyes when you are ready.

Exercise 1: Journal Capture

Take out your journal and quickly write whatever you would like to capture from this meditation. It could be a revelation, a reflection, a fleeting thought, or sensory perception.

Exercise 2: Self Qualities Journal Questions

After you've done the Self Qualities meditation and written your quick Journal Capture, take some time to explore more deeply by responding to the following journal prompts.

1. Which intentions resonate with you?
2. Which ones do you want to live into?
3. Were there any intentions you found difficult or challenging to relate to?
4. Did any part become activated?
5. Which parts keep you from living into the intentions you'd like to?
6. When a part gets activated, which intentions can you lean in to?

Exercise 3: Self Qualities Practice & Awareness

Over the next week, see if you can notice when you experience qualities of Self when interacting with others and/or with your parts. Make notes on your experience in the space below or in your journal.

Quality of Self	Describe your experience	What are your impressions?
Compassion		
Curiosity		
Calm		
Connectedness		
Confidence		
Courage		
Clarity		
Creativity		

CHAPTER 5

Be With

Encouraging Parts to Separate from You

I can't catch my breath. The pain in my chest is excruciating. It feels like someone is taking a sledgehammer to my ribcage from the inside and also like my heart is in a vise grip. I'm certain I will pass out. If I don't die from falling and hitting my head on the shower tile, this pain in my chest will take me out. The more I try to breathe, the tighter the grip on my heart. I'm sweating profusely. The pace of my heartbeat reaches a dizzying speed that causes nausea. I start to believe this is how my life ends, here in the shower, naked and defenseless. My brain tells me to call out to my husband for help, but trying to speak is met with a twisting chest pain that steals my words. The hot steam of the shower is suffocating. I am immobilized except for the tears flowing down my face. My internal temperature skyrockets, and the dizziness intensifies. The inevitable is about to happen. I hold the shower wall to steady myself. Just before I pass out, a thought flashes,

"You've experienced this before. Panic. You're not going to pass out or die. This is a panic attack."

I hear a compassionately soft voice say, "I can be with you and support you if you make room for me. Let me be with you." My body responds with shortness of breath and blurred vision. The voice continues in soft tones of a whisper, "I'm here with you; you're not alone. You don't have to do this by yourself." The voice seems a million miles away, and I desperately want to believe it. As it repeats itself several times, I am able to deepen my inhales and slow my exhales. Each time I do, the voice is clearer and closer. However, the pain in my chest and rapid heartbeat remain the same. My right hand moves to my heart, affirming that I am not alone, which slows my breath further. Next, I hear the voice say, "That's good, keep with the full breaths." The panic continues to abate. The voice goes on to say, "I'm with you. You're okay. Just breathe."

Now I (Self) have clarity that I'm speaking with Antsy as she is experiencing sheer panic. Being recognized by me, Antsy turns down the intensity of the chest pain and slightly slows the heartbeat. I (Self) thank Antsy for reducing the intensity of the bodily sensations. My hand remains on my heart as she unblends from me, and I can now be with her.

IFS CONCEPT 1: BLENDING

The way parts embody our systems is called *blending*. In the experience I've just shared, I was blended with Antsy. She took over my system, and her primary expression was in intense bodily sensations of shortness of breath, accelerated heart rate, chest pains, nausea, dizziness, panting, and blurred vision. When blending happens, access to our Self-energy is minimized. The part that is blended is in the seat of consciousness, and we experience the part as ourselves in totality, not as separate from us or a part of us. When Antsy was blended with my Self in this moment, I experienced her as *me*.

Parts blend with us as a way of communicating. When we are blended, the extreme feelings, thoughts, and beliefs of the part are what we experience. Antsy used my body to express her fear through intense somatic symptoms, which felt like dying.

Blending is a way parts express their needs. Although she didn't come right out and ask for what she needed, Antsy's fear was an indication of an unmet need. I later came to know she needed safety, connection, and to be understood. In Chapter 6, I talk about how to get to know our parts by befriending them.

IFS CONCEPT 2: UNBLENDING

Before we can get to know a part, the part must first unblend. When a part is in the seat of consciousness, we are that part. There is no separation between us and the part. Unblending is how parts create separation. We want parts to separate because this increases Self-energy and allows Self to come into relationship with the part. The part cannot be known if it is alone. The part needs to experience and be supported by Self to be heard, understood, and validated. Unblending allows Self to get to know the part. However, the part must unblend from Self, not the other way around; Self cannot drive the unblending. It must be the part's choice and the part's actions that cause unblending to happen. With unblending, the system shifts from being led by the part to Self-leadership.

In the story I just shared, the unblending process begins with Antsy, when Self reminds her that she has experienced these feelings in the past, names them as a panic attack, and reassures her that she is not going to die. Self goes on to request that Antsy make space for Self to support her so she doesn't have to be alone. Notice that Antsy doesn't completely unblend at the first request; she doesn't need to. Self just needs some separation to happen. Enough space is made that Self can continue to support Antsy by being present and reminding her over and over that she is not alone.

I have found that my parts respond well to physical connection, so one of the techniques my Self uses to calm my parts when they become dysregulated is touch. To assist Antsy in regulating, Self places its right hand over Antsy's fast-beating heart, deepening the connection between the two while creating a stabilizing presence for Antsy. The physical connection allows Antsy to slow her heart rate and encourages her to unblend further, giving Self greater presence in the system. Once that happens, Self can support and begin to get to know Antsy, understand the reason for the panic, and address her needs.

IFS CONCEPT 3: WHEN A PART DOESN'T UNBLEND

Some parts have a difficult time unblending. Even Antsy unblended only partially at first; her breathing slowed while her chest pains and rapid heartbeat persisted. However, there was enough separation for her to have awareness of Self. If Antsy had not responded to Self's support to unblend, that would have alerted Self that while gripped in a terrifying experience, Antsy was also afraid to separate. Self would have asked her, "What are you afraid would happen if you separated?" The primary fear parts have about separating is that I will somehow be harmed or something worse than what they are doing (in this case causing a panic attack) will happen to me. The parts' job is to keep me safe. If a part is afraid of losing its job, we first want to validate its importance in the system, then let the part know that we are not trying to get rid of it but want to get to know it, emphasizing that we cannot get to know it unless it allows us to be with it.

Protectors are diligent in their roles and do not want the system to experience the pain of the vulnerable parts they protect. They fear that if they separate, we will feel the intense feelings of worthlessness, not being good enough, or shame. If this is the part's fear, Self can ask the vulnerable part not to overwhelm the system with its intense feelings and beliefs while Self is getting to know it, and if the vulnerable part does express with intensity, Self can let the part know that Self only needs to experience a small amount of what it's feeling in order to understand. The main messages in addressing the protector's fears are that the protector controls the process, and it can come back to protect at any time. Letting the protector know that Self is not trying to change it or get rid of it allows it to relax and increases its willingness to unblend.

When the part's fears are sufficiently addressed and the part unblends, Self can notice any changes in thoughts, beliefs, emotions, and/or bodily sensations. Sometimes as our parts give space, the way they express themselves changes. In the opening story, Antsy's activation calmed more and more as her fear of dying was attended to. Acknowledge the change, and if the change provides relief, offer gratitude. Once the part unblends, let it know that you want to understand its experiences and get to know it better.

When parts are blended, they believe they are you. They have no awareness of a Self who can support them and handle what they believe you cannot. The key to helping our parts is assisting them to unblend. Self cannot make a part unblend; that is the part's choice, but Self can encourage the process. Parts are usually willing to unblend after they experience some quality of Self-energy. When the part separates, Self can be with the part. When parts refuse to separate, exploring and addressing their fears related to unblending is necessary. Until their fears are adequately addressed, parts will not feel safe enough to unblend.

Meditation: Be With

Note: This is a meditation created without the direct assistance of my ancestors.

The Be With meditation highlights the importance of parts unblending as essential to building relationship with parts and healing them. It also shows how being aware of what it's like in our system when we're blended with a part, versus when we're not, builds trust between Self and parts as parts get to experience being known by Self and knowing Self.

This meditation allows you to experience being blended, unblending, and experiencing the difference between being a part and being *with* a part.

Take a moment to get comfortable.
Close your eyes or soften your gaze.
Take note of your breath.
As you breathe, allow your awareness to follow the breath.
Continue to follow your breath to help you settle.

Bring to mind a situation that recently activated one of your parts.

It could be a disagreement you had with someone, a situation that caused annoyance, disbelief, anger, or anything else.

Allow the part to embody as if the situation is occurring now.

What do you notice?

What emotions are you experiencing?

What bodily sensations are present?

What are you saying?

What do you believe about the situation or person?

What are your thoughts?

Let whatever is coming up completely embody you, and stay with what you're experiencing.

Ask the part to separate from you. It can do so by:

Stepping outside of you slightly.

Sitting next to you.

Decreasing its emotions.

Turning down the intensity of body sensations.

If the part unblends, notice what it feels likes to be separate from the part.

Just be with the part in this separate and connected state.

If the part does not unblend, ask, "What are you afraid will happen if you separate?"

Listen to the part's fears.

Address any fears the part shares with you.

After addressing the part's fears, ask it to separate now.

If it separates now, notice what you feel.

If it still doesn't unblend, continue to identify and address its fears.

If your part did unblend, continue to be with the part.

Take note of the difference between the part being blended and now unblended.

How do you feel toward the part in this unblended state?

If you feel one of the qualities of Self-energy, send that energy to the part.

How does the part respond to the Self-energy?

Set an intention to come back to your part at a later time.

Thank your part. If it was able to separate, thank it for doing so.

If it was not able to separate, thank it for sharing its fears with you.

Bring your awareness to your breath, and when it feels right, re-enter this moment and space by slowly opening your eyes when you're ready.

Exercise 1: Journal Capture

Journal what you would like to capture from this meditation, like a revelation, reflection, or anything significant you want to remember from this experience.

Exercise 2: Be With Journal Questions

After you've done the Be With meditation and written your quick Journal Capture, take some time to explore more deeply by responding to the following journal prompts.

1. Describe the activating situation or person.
2. What was your experience of being blended with your part?
    a. Emotions
    b. Bodily sensations
    c. What the part said
    d. Beliefs
    e. Thoughts
    f. Anything else
3. How did your part respond to being asked to unblend?
4. If your part did unblend, what did you experience after it separated from you?
5. If your part did not unblend, what were its fears?

6. How did your part respond to Self-energy?
7. What intentions did you set with your part?

Exercise 3: Activation Practice

This exercise helps to notice parts in real time and to unblend them in the moments of activation. Being with parts will assist in developing relationship and trust between them and Self.

1. Over the next week, check in with the part from the meditation daily.
2. Pay attention to when this part is present.
3. Track the situations and/or people that activate this part in your daily life.
4. When this part is present, ask it to unblend so you can be with it in its activation.
5. Journal about your experience with this part daily and what you learned.

CHAPTER 6

Crystal Cave with the Ancestors

Building Relationships with Your Parts

In the last chapter, we met my part Antsy. We learned of her struggle to unblend, as she thought she was alone and had no awareness of Self. She was eventually able to unblend, and now we pick up her story from her separated state as Self befriends her.

The first thing I do after Antsy unblends is extend compassion toward her. I want her to experience what I feel for her. I extend curiosity too, because I am genuinely interested in the root of her panicked state. I begin to deepen our connection by silently being with Antsy, with my hand on my heart, allowing her to feel my presence with her.

Compassionately I ask, "What's causing you panic right now?" Antsy responds, "It's terrifying to get everything I've always wanted. I'm terrified. This is so scary for me." A torrent of Antsy's tears streams down my face with this revelation. I experience it as an emotional release of what she has been holding as she acknowledges her terror out loud. I tell Antsy that she doesn't have to be alone in her fear. I reassure her that I am with her and will not leave her. I reassure her that she doesn't have to do anything. I can be with her and handle what terrifies her. I assure her that if she remains separate from me like she is right now in the face of what scares her, I can support her as she moves forward. She responds with an audible sigh, which causes my body to relax even more. The chest pain, although still present, lessens, and the fast heartbeat and grip are less intense. She says, "I didn't know you were here. I thought I had to handle what comes next by myself."

Antsy reminds me of the significant achievements I've accomplished in the past two years. The last two of my five children were launched. My husband and I embarked on a dream, seven years in the making, of becoming permanent international travelers. I achieved the goal of becoming an IFS Solo lead trainer after a five-year process, and I signed a contract with Hay House for the publication of this book.

"All of this goodness reminds me of the fear I felt when graduating from college with plans to pursue a master's degree in social work," Antsy tells me. "Do you remember how scary that was?"

"Yes, I do remember your panic back then. What's the connection between now and then?"

"I want you to be successful. I want you to fulfill your dreams and goals, and it scares me when you do."

"I'm not sure I'm understanding the connection between wanting me to succeed and getting fearful when I do."

Antsy takes a deep breath in and lets out a loud sigh. "I cause you to feel anxious when we begin a goal. I do this because I want to push you to get what you set out to achieve. I want to motivate you to stay on track, to not stop. The anxiety is there so you don't lose sight of what you want."

Nodding, I say, "It sounds like you become invested in my goal and work hard to support me in getting there."

"Yeah, but when you achieve many things at once, I become overwhelmed and panicky, like now. I worry that you're reaching for too much and you'll fail. I panic because I'm terrified of your failure. My job is to help you achieve."

When Antsy shares this, I feel the emotion of another part coming to the surface. Tears well in my eyes. This other part is the exile that Antsy protects by keeping busy helping me achieve. I turn my attention calmly to the exile and say, "I feel you here. I promise I'll come back and talk with you. Can you relax back and allow space for me to spend more time with Antsy?" I feel the desperation of this little one as it softens back.

"Tell me more about your terror of my failure."

"Maybe it's my failure I'm afraid of. Maybe I'm afraid I will fail at keeping you adequately motivated. You're always reaching for the next big thing, and I don't know that I can keep up with your bigger and grander goals."

"Antsy, when did you start motivating me in this way?"

"Probably when you were in elementary school."

Interestedly, I ask, "What was going on during elementary school to cause you to use anxiety as a way to motivate me?"

"I noticed that everyone around you responded positively when you achieved. Your parents were happy and proud and showed you love. Your teachers supported and encouraged your success. So I wanted more of those good feelings for you."

"Antsy, I'm wondering what you're afraid would happen if you did not cause anxiety and panic."

"Failure!" Antsy shouts.

"Okay, what are you afraid would happen if we failed?"

Antsy sits quietly, with her arms crossed, as she thinks. When she speaks, her voice is much lower. "I'm afraid that if we failed, no one would see you as valuable, and you'd be unlovable and alone."

Over time, I have gained clarity that Antsy's role in my system is achievement. She does an excellent job of creating a level of anxiety to motivate me to keep moving toward my goals. However, she experiences what feels like life-threatening panic when major goals are achieved. At these times, she finds herself in a transitional space of not knowing what I will pursue next and, more importantly, whether she can measure up to the next challenge. She uses my entire body to communicate her terror of failure. Antsy believes I receive love by achieving. Ultimately, she is protecting me from feeling unlovable and being alone. The only way to learn the true purpose behind the extreme behaviors and beliefs of our parts is to come into relationship with them through befriending. When we show them genuine interests, they feel seen and valued, which encourages them to trust us enough to share.

IFS CONCEPT 1: BEFRIEND

Befriending is getting to know a part by interacting with it and building a Self-to-part relationship. Parts are leading the system because they lack awareness of Self or, if they do have awareness, they don't trust Self. Therefore, our protectors continue in the extreme roles they have taken on because they believe they don't have any other choice. They do not know they can rely on Self as a resource to guide, support, and heal. Before Self can befriend a part, there needs to be awareness of the part in or around the body. We have to notice the part before we can come into relationship with it. Once there is a sense of the part, we may have to ask the part to unblend or separate from us, allowing us to come into relationship with it. We know Self is preparing to befriend the part and not another part, when we experience one of the qualities of Self, compassion, curiosity, calm, connectedness, clarity, confidence, courage, or creativity toward the part. If we feel something other than a Self quality, then another part is present, and we need to ask that part to step back. For example, when I felt the energy of the young exile while working with Antsy, I asked that part to step back and allow Antsy and me more time.

When we experience one of the eight Cs, or essential qualities of Self, toward a part, we want to share that energy with the part by directing it toward the part. If we're feeling connected to the part, we want to energetically share that connectedness with the part. Often, the part will relax or express curiosity or interest in us. We want to extend the energy of Self until we notice some change in the part. This may happen quickly, or it may take some time. If we are feeling compassion or curiosity or any other quality in addition to connection, we want to extend that energy too. This is especially true if the part is skeptical of Self or takes longer to relax in the presence of Self. Proximity also helps parts connect with Self. If the part is at a distance or has its back turned or seems disinterested, moving physically closer to the part while extending the energy of one of the eight Cs may open the part to the presence of Self.

There are several ways to deepen the befriending process. When we extend the quality of Self toward the part, we want to notice how the part responds. This provides information about how interested the part is in connecting with us. Does the part relax or ignore us? Do we get the sense that a different part is present? We want the part to notice Self. If the part has no awareness of Self before this interaction, it may take it a while to acknowledge or understand what is happening. We want to allow time for the part to feel our presence with it. We can slow down and take our time at this point and be with the part in a way that feels right for the part. Different parts of us will need different amounts and kinds of connection and energy from Self. They are not one-size-fits-all parts. However, because of the intuitive nature of Self, we will know how to engage our parts, giving them what they need in the present. Once the part notices Self, relaxes, or seems interested, we let the part know we want to get to know it better. As the part shares about itself, we want to express genuine curiosity, validating and demonstrating compassion for the part's experiences. We also want to learn how the part protects us. The conversation with the part is not one-sided. We can say what we would like to say or ask of the part.

Let's turn back to Antsy. When she separated or unblended from me by decreasing the intensity of somatic sensations, I (Self) was able to befriend her. To recap: I started by expressing curiosity about the cause of Antsy's panic. I learned that she was terrified as I reached several significant life goals within a two-year period. Achieving the goal of successfully raising and launching five children with my husband allowed us to pursue the dream life of traveling internationally full-time. I had pursued the goal of writing a book for over 20 years and the goal of becoming an IFS Lead Trainer for five years. With these major accomplishments coming to fruition, Antsy's terror of failure was amplified. She seemed to express anxiety while in pursuit of a goal, but panicked when the goal was attained.

As Self befriended Antsy, she experienced the presence of Self more fully. In a Self-led way, I continued to encourage her to calm and reassure her that she was safe. The placing of the hand on the heart was another way that Self let Antsy know she was not alone. Self is intuitive and had a sense that touch would deepen the connection with Antsy and help her to calm. Touch is a very powerful comforter for some parts. If touch is something your parts respond positively to, use it to support the unblending and befriending process. If not, that's okay too. The use of a calming voice with words of reassurance is the basis for building a trusting relationship with parts.

Self continued to befriend Antsy, allowing her to experience qualities of Self-energy. The qualities shared with Antsy were compassion, curiosity, calm, and connectedness. Self also took its time with her; there was no rush for her to do something or change states. During the befriending process, we learned about Antsy's experiences, which encouraged the relationship to deepen. Self continued to express compassion with curiosity as it began to inquire about what is causing the panic. Self offered more acceptance and reassurance after Antsy shared her fears. She was encouraged to remain separate in times of high fear in order to be in relationship with Self, who can support her through the fear and panic about what comes next.

Self can only befriend parts after they unblend. Antsy did not quickly unblend; she did so with the reassuring support of Self. However, parts don't always unblend even with encouragement and patience. When this happens, Self needs to discover and address the reasons parts won't unblend. Unblending is necessary to befriend our parts.

IFS CONCEPT 2: FLESH OUT

Fleshing out is how we get to know more about our parts and build a deeper, trusting relationship between them and Self. Once we befriend a part, we can ask the part what it would like to share about itself and its experiences. I think about fleshing out as how we might engage a dear friend as they share something difficult about their life or history. We would listen, ask questions based on what they are sharing, show interest and care. This is what Self does: it supports the unfolding of the part's story and sharing. Self does a good job reflecting to the part the hardship, pain, confusion, overwhelm, or anything else the part is experiencing.

Validation and understanding are important in fleshing out. When parts feel seen by Self, we can find out their role in the system, how they took on their current role, and what they hope to accomplish. These questions often point to an early wounding experienced by us. Which leads to who the part is protecting and informs Self where healing can occur.

IFS CONCEPT 3: DIRECT ACCESS

Up to this point, I have shared how to notice, get to know, and befriend parts from your Self. In IFS, this is called In-sight. In-sight is hyphenated to highlight that it is the seeing or sight that happens when we go inside. Parts come into relationship with you (your Self), building a Self-to-part relationship. There's another way to connect with parts that requires working with another person, usually a therapist, practitioner, or coach. This technique is called Direct Access. Instead of you coming into relationship with your parts, the therapist or other professional builds a Self-to-part relationship with your parts using *their* Self. This involves you blending with the part or becoming the part, allowing the therapist to speak directly with your part. Direct Access is most beneficial with parts that don't trust you or have no awareness of Self (you). Direct Access allows these parts an opportunity to experience the healing power of Self outside of your system. This usually results in parts being open to connecting with you after interacting with a compassionate other in the Self of the therapist. The goals of Direct Access are to validate the part, to be curious about its experiences, to address its fears, and build trust. Once the part feels heard and its concerns have been adequately addressed, it is more willing and likely to unblend and come into relationship with you.

The following case vignette is an example of the use of Direct Access to befriend a part with suicidal thoughts and actions. Since IFS holds that all parts have positive intentions, a key factor in befriending parts that think about harm and/or act on these thoughts is to discover their positive intentions.

Case Vignette: The Suicidal Part

When I met Fern, she was estranged from her family of origin for several years. She identifies as biracial with a Black mother and white father. She never met her biological father and was raised by a stepfather who is also white. Fern came for therapy with severe depression and suicidal thoughts. She has a history of traumatic sexual abuse by her stepfather and his brother. The depth of her despair and worthlessness filled the therapy room. Fern has attempted suicide multiple times since childhood and experienced more hospitalizations than she could give an accurate count of.

I believe therapists are most activated by parts that want to hurt or kill the client. With Fern, we worked with such a part—her part that considers suicide and has attempted suicide on multiple occasions.

When Fern arrives at the session, she is already blended with this part that views suicide as an option to her despair and depression. She sits crumpled on the couch.

"Nothing is ever going to change," Fern's suicidal part says. "I've tried everything. The pain is never going to stop."

"I hear that things feel hopeless right now," I offer.

"Hopeless, dark, unending. I need the pain to end, it's too much."

"Tell me more about the pain being too much," I inquire softly.

"It feels like being on a medieval torture rack being twisted and stretched to the point of excruciating pain. Why would I want to stick around for more of that?"

"Maybe you want to stick around because a small part of you has a glimmer of hope," I say compassionately.

"Hope has let me down a thousand times. Hope is useless. I know a sure way out of this pain."

"So, what I'm hearing is you want the pain to stop, right?"

"I can't. I can't keep suffering like this," Fern shakes her head with closed eyes. "I've tried to stop the pain with pills, drugs, and cutting many times, but it didn't work. Someone always saves me. For what? For me to survive to endure the same agony. No one can fix this for me. Only I can."

"Wow, that makes so much sense. Your goal is not to hurt, and the way you accomplish that is by killing yourself."

The part nods and smiles.

"What if I could offer another way to stop your pain without hurting or killing yourself. Would you be interested?"

The part looks both confused and curious. "Maybe, but I don't think there is any other way."

"I know you don't, but would you be willing to try?"

Slowing, with emphasis on each word, the part says, "I . . . only . . . want . . . to. . . stop . . . hurting!"

"Is that a yes?" I ask, because I want to be certain before moving forward.

"Yes, I'll try."

After using Direct Access and receiving buy-in from the part, my work with Fern moves into a new phase. I encourage the part to unblend from Fern and come into relationship with Fern's Self. Once the part unblends, I support Fern in befriending the part to increase the trust between the part and Fern's Self. With trust established, we work toward healing the exile the suicidal part protects.

Meditation: Crystal Cave with the Ancestors

As I spent more time getting to know my ancestors in my mother's mother's line, they continued to support me in learning the IFS model by offering meditations inspired by the model. I found this extremely surprising. I wondered, "How do they know my heart so clearly and offer precisely what I need to achieve my goals?" What I learned is our ancestors love us immensely and conspire for our highest good. To this end, my ancestors led me to work with my most challenging parts by drawing on the Self-energy of my ancestral lines.

This meditation is offered to provide the additional support of ancestor wisdom and Self-energy to support you when working with parts you struggle with.

Adjust your body until it feels comfortable.

Close your eyes or soften your gaze.

Notice how your body connects with the surface that supports you.

Inhale from the bottom of your feet, bringing the breath up through your body.

Exhale through your body and out the bottom of your feet.

Do this a few times.

Picture yourself hiking or walking in a canyon, admiring the breathtaking sites along your way.

During your trek, you get caught in a downpour.

Looking around for a place to wait out the rain, you see a cave.

As you focus on the entrance through the cascading water, you see an ancestor waving for you to join them.

Dashing for the cave, you duck inside.

Your ancestor accompanies you deeper inside the darkened space until you see a faint light in the distance.

Curiously you take in your surroundings. Your eyes are drawn to the walls of the cave, and you notice colorful, luminous crystals embedded there.

When your eyes fully adjust to the limited lighting, you see a second ancestor seated on the floor.

This ancestor welcomes you and invites you and the ancestor who greeted you at the entrance to sit with them.

Take a moment to visually capture how your ancestors look.

The ancestor who was in the cave says, "We are here to help you with a part of yourself you struggle with. Notice this part and invite it to join us wherever it feels comfortable."

The ancestor who greeted you says, "We have seen you wrestle with this part and come to offer wisdom from your ancestral line to support you as you work with this part of yourself."

The ancestors encourage you to draw on their energy to increase the Self energy in space if you need to.

Then the three of you sit with the part emanating Self-energy toward the part.

The ancestors take turns with questions to help you get to know this part.

The first ancestor encourages you to ask the part, "How do you help me?"

The second ancestor asks you to ask the part, "How did you start helping me in this way?"

Next, you're instructed to ask, "How long have you been doing this for me?"

The next question you hear is, "What are you trying to accomplish by doing this for me?"

The first ancestor suggests asking, "Do you like what you're doing?"

Next you hear, "Ask the part what it would rather do if it didn't need to protect you in this way."

Lastly, one of the ancestors asks, "Is there anything you want to say to this part?"

The ancestor gets up, walks to the illuminated wall, and slowly moves their hands over the colorful crystals, pauses at one, and retrieves it.

The ancestor hands the crystal to you, saying, "This crystal will help crystallize what you learned here. Take note of the size, weight, shape, color, and vibration as it represents your part."

The other ancestor asks, "Is there anything you want to ask or say to us?"

After this exchange, your ancestors offer to walk you back to the entrance of the cave.

As you get closer to the opening, you see the sun shining brightly, lighting your way.

If you would like to, set an intention with your ancestors and the part represented by the crystal.

When that feels complete, bring your awareness to your breath, and just breathe as you re-enter this moment and space.

Slowly open your eyes when you are ready.

Exercise 1: Journal Capture

Journal what you would like to capture from this meditation, like a revelation, reflection, or anything significant you want to remember from this experience.

Exercise 2: Crystal Cave with the Ancestors Journal Questions

After you've done the Crystal Cave with the Ancestors meditation and written your quick Journal Capture, take some time to explore more deeply by responding to the following journal prompts.

1. What was your experience with your ancestors?
2. Which part did you befriend?
3. What did you learn from the part?
4. How has what you learned impacted how you view this part?
5. What would the part rather do than protect you in the way that it does?
6. Describe the crystal given to you by the ancestor that represents this part?
7. Who were the two ancestors? Describe them.

Exercise 3: Deepening the Relationship

1. How can you deepen the relationship with the part you met with in the cave?
2. How might your ancestors assist you in deepening the relationship with the part?
3. How will you deepen your relationship with your ancestors?

CHAPTER 7

Polarization Picnic

Parts with Opposing Views

Survive: "I can't believe you're even considering closing your therapy practice. What are you thinking? How will you make it? You'll starve. You need to be rational about this. Why change what's working? Just leave well enough alone."

Thrive: "You can't keep working at this pace. You're trying to maintain a full-time practice and become a trainer. It's like you're working two full-time jobs. This is killing you. You can't hold on to your old life and create the new one at the same time. If you're worried about finances, don't. You'll be fine."

Survive: "It won't be fine. Bills don't get paid by themselves. We don't have a crystal ball. There's no guarantee this trainer thing will work out. We need to stick with what we know. You know what you're doing works. You've spent years building your practice. Don't walk away. And what about your clients? They need you."

Thrive: "Refuse to move in fear. Survive's decisions are based on fear. Trust the plan. You said you wanted to build a flourishing practice focusing on consultation, training, workshops/retreats, writing, and speaking. I believe it will be more successful than your therapy practice. To make this dream a reality, you have to close your practice. That's the only way."

Survive: "Yeah, yeah, yeah! But that's all future promise that may or may not happen. Please don't throw away what you've worked so hard to create. You have been doing this for 10 years and you want to throw it all away for the unknown. That's foolish!"

Thrive: "We've taken risks before and reaped great benefits. We took a risk when you left your job as a hospital social worker to open your practice, and look what we built. Survive tried to convince you not to leave the comforts of that job too. Now that this has become comfortable, he doesn't want you to aim higher."

Survive: "I think you're making a mistake if you listen to Thrive. He is a risk-taker, and great, the last time worked out, but we struggled for a time before it worked out. We're comfortable; things are stable and profitable. Why start over again? Why? I say we leave things as they are."

Thrive: "We've already done the private practice thing. It's time to spread our wings and have a greater impact on the field. You believe in IFS therapy and want to bring it to as many people as possible. I can help you to do that. Sure, it will be uncomfortable for a while, but the discomfort will be brief, just as it was when you were building your private practice. I say close your psychotherapy practice and focus on becoming an IFS trainer and consultant."

Have you ever had two voices in your head telling you to do two completely different things? Well, that was my experience with Survive and Thrive. I had a successful private practice, and I was being mentored toward becoming an

IFS trainer. I came to a point in the process where exhaustion was setting in because, essentially, I had two full-time jobs. I found myself at a crossroads. It was no longer possible for me to continue with both in the same manner. I found that the trainer track required much more from me than I could have predicted, and I was committed to giving this new career path my full attention and effort. So I was faced with a decision to close my psychotherapy practice or significantly reduce my caseload to continue my pursuit of becoming the first Black IFS Solo lead trainer.

Thrive and Survive continued to bicker and were unwilling to compromise. They each held that their position was the best solution. When one tried to convince me to side with them, the other strongly opposed and argued for their point of view. This dynamic is referred to as polarization.

IFS CONCEPT 1: POLARIZATION

Polarization is what happens when two or more parts hold differing and sometimes opposite positions. Often these parts have little access to Self. They are so focused on their viewpoint and not allowing the other part to take over that they do not notice the availability of Self. Their hyper-focus on preventing the other from taking over keeps them in a vicious loop of maintaining balance by not giving in or even considering a compromise.

Experiencing polarization is common, since most of our parts are polarized with another part. The polarization can be experienced as fear, dislike, or disagreement between parts. The most common polarizations are between protectors, such as manager/firefighter, manager/manager, and firefighter/firefighter. However parts can also be polarized with exiles. Polarized protectors are like people who hold differing views and opinions. Protectors do not want the opposing view to dominate the system, so they do their best to ensure that their position prevails. These polarized parts function usually to protect a vulnerable part or exile, and they can serve as distractions from deeper emotions or pain. Ultimately, these parts want the same outcome, but their tactics differ. The goal is to attend to each view equally to understand what parts need and what they are attempting to do.

IFS CONCEPT 2: WORKING WITH POLARIZED PARTS

The first step in working with a polarization is identifying the parts involved. We want to understand the relationship between the polarized parts. Is one part fearful of another? Are parts in a struggle with one another? Are parts reacting to each other in some way? We want to identify the parts on either side of the polarization, keeping in mind there can be more than two parts involved in a polarization; in that case, a coalition of parts exists on either side.

As an example, a coalition of people-pleasing parts could include a part that goes along to get along, another part that keeps quiet as a way to please others, and another part that allows others to use it as a doormat. The other side of the polarization may include a coalition of parts that get angry to protect. This coalition has a part that gets angry at the people-pleasing parts, another part that gets angry at the object of the people-pleasing parts, and a third part that criticizes everyone involved. Remember, the biggest fear of polarized parts, or coalitions of parts, is the other side dominating and taking over. It is important when working with a polarization to address this fear by letting each part know that you will not allow the other side to take over and you will hear from each part.

Again, when we begin working with a polarization, we consider every part involved. (To simplify the process, I will use the example of two polarized parts instead of a coalition; however, the same steps apply when working with a coalition.)

First, we want to focus on both sides of the polarization at the same time. To help us do this, we can notice how each part shows up in or around the body, we can draw each part on a sheet of paper, or we can imagine holding one part in each hand.

Let's take the example of noticing how each part shows up in or around the body. I noticed that Thrive showed up outside of my body on the left side, impatient and eager to move forward. He used his hands and body to punctuate his words. Survive expressed as a nervous pit in my stomach. After sensing how each part reveals itself, we want to notice how we feel toward each part. We might notice parts that align with either side of the polarized pair or parts that have an agenda. If those parts are present, we ask them to step back. Once those parts unblend, we want to notice how we feel toward each part of the polarization again. When we unblend from parts, what remains is Self. We continue to check how we feel toward the parts until we have Self energy toward each part of the polarization.

If we feel one or more of the qualities of Self (compassion, curiosity, calm, confidence, creativity, connectedness, courage, or clarity), we can energetically extend that quality of Self to one or both parts.

If we feel something other than these qualities, it means that another part is present, so we ask it to step back (unblend).

After extending qualities of Self, we ask permission to get to know each side of the polarization. This means we ask each side not to blend or take over while getting to know the other side. If one side has more energy, that may be the part we talk to first. If the energy of the parts is similar, ask the parts who would like to share first, reminding them that each will have their turn.

In getting to know each part, we want to learn their role in the system. What do they do, and what are they trying to accomplish? Since all parts have positive intentions, we know these parts are attempting to help, and we want to discover their positive intentions. We want to know how this struggle is working for them. Oftentimes, struggle between the parts does not result in them getting what they want. Asking these questions helps the parts to see the results of their efforts. They may not have noticed that they're not getting the outcomes they want because they have been too focused on the struggle with each other.

After getting to know one side of the polarization, spend time asking the same questions of the other part. In this way, each side gets to learn how the other side is trying to help and protect you. When the parts realize each other's role and that neither is getting their desired outcome, they usually soften and calm.

Next, we want to get curious about whom the polarized parts protect. Often, we discover they are protecting the same exiled part. Even though they may be using different methods and strategies, they are doing the same job. This revelation can open the parts to trying something new instead of continuing in their struggle. We want to take time to understand what each part is afraid would happen if they stopped protecting in the way they do. We will find our parts protect ferociously because they do not want us to experience the pain the exile is holding. When we know their fears and who they protect, we can offer to heal the one they protect if they are interested and give permission. If permission is granted, we can begin to build a Self-to-part relationship with the exile and heal it using the steps in Chapter 10.

It is important to note that even after getting polarized parts to relax and calm, they will not stop protecting until the one they protect is healed (unburdened). However, they now have a relationship with Self that they did not have previously. We can ask parts to trust Self to address the problem that concerns them. After the exile is unburdened, the polarized parts can take on different roles in the system because they will not need to protect the exile in the same manner after it is healed. We can have them talk and listen to each other with Self as a mediator. This will help them decide on new roles that could somehow include working together as allies instead of adversaries fearing domination by the other.

Case Vignette: Go Along to Get Along vs. Bulldog

Angel is a 39-year-old, well-educated, successful female Nigerian immigrant working in international finance. She came to therapy for anxiety. She was experiencing constant worry, inability to focus on work, nervousness, sleeplessness, and irritability. She believed her symptoms were the result of racialized workplace trauma.

In our session, Angel describes her immediate boss's low and derogatory views of people of color. She shares that her boss constantly compares her to other Black employees she has managed in the past. Her boss gives what she considers compliments, but Angel experiences them as stressful microaggressions: for example, "You're highly driven for a Black person," or "You're not lazy like the other Black women who've worked for me," or "You're a real pack mule when it comes to how many projects you can manage."

Angel says that although her workplace was toxic to begin with, her anxiety became impossible to manage when she was overlooked for a promotion after doing the job for six months without a title or pay increase, and while possessing more education, experience, and qualifications than the person who was ultimately selected for the position. When I asked Angel about her experiences at work and her anxiety, I immediately met her polarized parts.

"I am by far the most qualified for the promotion. I hold degrees from two Ivy League universities. I spent six months doing the job required of the position. I've taken on every project my boss has offered, carrying a much higher workload than my co-workers. I want to say something about not getting the promotion, but it's better not to rock the boat and ruin my chances for future promotions."

"What would you want to know from your boss?"

"I want to know what I can do to improve my chances for promotion. I know how to give people exactly what they want from me. All she needs to do is tell me, and I'll deliver. But on the other hand, I deserve to know why I didn't get the damn promotion. No one else works their ass off the way I do. I've been doing the job for six months! I want to storm into her office and demand the truth. I tolerated her racist comments and microaggressions. I'm tired of it! I thought this promotion was a sure way to get out from under her thumb and to work in a new division in another office."

"Angel, I'm hearing that you're torn between not making waves and wanting to demand answers. It also sounds like you feel slighted and angry after doing the job for six months, is that correct?"

"Yes." After a long pause she adds, "And no. I want to know why she didn't promote the most qualified person on her team. I want to know if I'm wasting my time. But if I ask, I'm afraid I'll never get promoted. I can wait. I will wait. Then I think, this is bullshit! I have worked hard and proven my value. Yet it is the white men on the team who get promoted. To add insult to being overlooked, she asked me to bring the white man who got promoted up to speed. I am so damn angry. I don't know who I'm most angry with, her or myself." Angel closes her eyes, shakes her head, and sighs in disbelief.

"I hear how hard you're working and not being recognized for your contribution. I get a sense that you're most angry about tolerating your boss's microaggressions and still not being promoted."

"Thank you for saying that, because sometimes I feel like I'm not seeing or experiencing what I am. When my boss comments that I'm different from other Black people she's managed—when she displays genuine surprise that I consistently arrive to work on time, complete projects on or ahead of schedule, and don't complain about my workload—I think it's going to pay off. I refuse to live down to her low expectations of me as a Black professional. The fact that she has such low expectations of me and other Black people pisses me off, but if I express my anger, I could lose my job. I even feel I'll lose my job if I ask why I didn't get promoted. I feel like I have no options but to keep doing what I've been doing: work hard and continue to take on the special projects, because if I keep demonstrating my worth, she'll take note."

"I hear you going back and forth between trying to please the boss by being a model employee, taking on extra projects and roles, and not being appreciated or rewarded for your dedication, which makes you angry."

"Yes, that's exactly it. I have my Go Along to Get Along part that wants to please everybody, and then I have the Bulldog who wants to fight for what's right."

"How do you feel toward these parts?"

"I don't like either."

"Angel, can you ask the part that doesn't like either to step back?"

"Oh, sure." She closes her eyes and speaks silently with that part.

"Now, how do you feel toward the Go Along to Get Along part and the Bulldog?"

"I want to understand them more. I'm curious about them both."

"Okay, that's good. Let the parts know you're curious and see if they're willing to get to know you and each other."

When Angel felt curious about both parts, they agreed to listen to each other and share their fears and concerns with her. We discovered that Go Along to Get Along is Angel's face to the world. This part assists her in succeeding in school, career, and relationships by insisting that she go along with what other people want and expect of her, even when she doesn't want to, because this part believes being likeable and not rocking the boat is how Angel will get ahead. Go Along to Get Along helps Angel to feel valued and seen by others by pleasing them and being likable. She also hopes that by appeasing others, she can keep Bulldog under control. Go Along to Get Along fears two outcomes if she stops doing her job. First, that Bulldog will blow up Angel's life and cause irrevocable damage. Second, that Angel will feel worthless and unlovable and this will result in her being alone.

In spending time getting to know Bulldog, we found there are two situations likely to activate this part's rage. This part is angered when it believes Angel is being victimized or allowing others to take advantage of her. Bulldog holds that Angel is responsible at least partly for what it views as mistreatment because she won't stand up for herself. It becomes enraged when Angel feels the emotional pain of worthlessness. In this particular situation, Bulldog was enraged and ready to confront Angel's boss for devaluing her and causing feelings of unworthiness to surface.

In this exchange, Angel gained valuable information that she didn't have before getting to know these parts. Her biggest takeaway was that neither part wanted her to feel worthless. They were both protecting the same exile. Go Along to Get Along protected Angel from feeling worthless by meeting others' needs and requests in order to prove her value. If others see her as invaluable, she will not feel worthless, this part reasons. Bulldog's strategy was to get angry, challenge, and criticize when Angel experienced worthlessness. Both Go Along to Get Along and Bulldog are protectors in Angel's system. Go Along to Get Along is a manager who is working to keep Angel from ever feeling the worthlessness of the exile, and Bulldog is a firefighter who springs into action when Angel feels devalued and worthless. When these two parts gained awareness of how similar their roles are, they relaxed and granted access to the exile they both protected.

Parts will give access to the vulnerable exile they protect when they feel heard. In the case of a polarization, the part needs to be heard and understood not only by the Self but also by the parts it's polarized with. If parts do not allow access to the exile, it means you need to take more time to get to know these parts. It is important to discover what they are afraid would happen if they let you connect with the one they protect. Again, you need to hear them out, express compassion and curiosity for their concerns. Sometimes, it is too difficult to access an exile on your own, and it may require professional help. (See "Still Listening Resources" at the end of this book to locate a therapist or practitioner if you need to.)

Meditation: Polarization Picnic

The Polarization Picnic meditation is the sixth given to me by my ancestors. At the time I received this, I had been going back and forth about whether it was time to significantly reduce my private practice caseload. My burgeoning IFS consultation business and my pursuit of becoming an IFS trainer were requiring significantly more attention and time. One day I had certainty about cutting back my practice, and the very next day, I'd convince myself not to. During this dilemma, my generous and wise ancestors gifted me with the Polarization Picnic meditation. By listening to each side of my polarization, I gained clarity and ultimately was able to make a Self-led decision about my practice.

This meditation invites you to get to know the story of two of your polarized parts, develop a relationship with them, and discover the vulnerable part they protect.

Find a comfortable seat.
Close your eyes or soften your gaze.
Bring your awareness to your breath and just breathe.
Breathe in for four counts and breathe out for four counts.
Do that a few times, increasing your relaxation.

Visualize you're in a park, sitting on a picnic blanket.

You have a picnic basket with a spread of your favorite foods, enough to feed you and several others.

While removing items from the basket, you hear arguing.

You look in the direction of the disagreeable noise and see two parts of yourself.

They are speaking in raised tones with neither listening.

You do what you can to get their attention.

When they notice, you invite them to join you on the blanket.

They sit down and start explaining their side of the argument.

Compassionately, you tell them you want to help.

Again, they respond by speaking over one another.

Share that you're curious to get to know each of them one at a time.

Reassure them that each will get a chance, and you will not allow one to take over.

Next, you ask them if they are willing to listen to each other.

If they are not, listen and address their concerns.

If they are, ask the first part why it is doing what it's doing.

Then ask how it is trying to help.

Once you have a sense of how this part is trying to help, turn to the second part and ask why it is doing what it's doing.

Now ask how it is trying to help.

Notice how both parts are trying to help you and acknowledge their positive intent.

Ask them what their behavior costs them.

Allow each an opportunity to speak in turn.

When that feels complete, ask each of them what they are afraid would happen if they didn't do this.

Lastly, ask them to show you the vulnerable one they are protecting.

If they do, let them know that you can help that part.

If they do not, that's okay. You may need to spend more time getting to know them.

Invite them to share your picnic meal, and over the meal, explore with the parts anything else they want to share with you.

Let them know you would like to continue connecting with them, and set intentions to do so.

If it feels right, show them some appreciation for what they shared with you and each other.

Bring your awareness to your breath and just breathe as you re-enter this moment and space.

Slowly open your eyes when you are ready.

Exercise 1: Journal Capture

Journal what you would like to capture from this meditation, like a revelation, reflection, or anything significant you want to remember from this experience.

Exercise 2: Polarization Picnic Journal Questions

After you've done the Polarization Picnic meditation and written your quick Journal Capture, take some time to explore more deeply by responding to the following journal prompts.

1. Who are your polarized parts?
2. Describe how your parts are polarized.
3. Were your parts able to listen to each other? Why? Why not?

4. What is the position of each part?
5. Why is each part doing what they are doing?
6. How is each part trying to help you?
7. Who is the vulnerable one(s) your parts protect?
8. What are the situations and/or people in your life that activate these parts?
9. What more did you learn from these parts?

Exercise 3: Drawing the Polarized System

Before starting this exercise, get some drawing supplies: paper, markers, colored pencils, paints, whatever works for you. Then move through the steps of this exercise.

Step 1: Go inside and connect with the first part from the Polarization Picnic meditation. It may express itself with words, images, sensations, emotions, or a felt sense.

Step 2: Once you have a sense of this part, ask it how it wants to be represented on the page, then draw it.

Step 3: Go inside and connect with the second part from the Polarization Picnic meditation.

Step 4: Once you have a sense of this part, ask it how it wants to be represented on the page and where it wants to be on the page in relationship to the first part, then draw it.

Step 5: Look at the first part you drew. How do you feel toward this part? If it is a quality of Self (compassion, curiosity, calm, confidence, creativity, connectedness, courage, or clarity), draw a representation of the quality of Self near the part. If it's not a quality of Self, connect with this new part and draw it on the page where it wants to be placed.

Step 6: Look at the second part you drew. How do you feel toward this part? If it is a quality of Self (compassion, curiosity, calm, confidence, creativity, connectedness, courage, or clarity), draw a representation of the quality of Self near the part. If it's not a quality of Self, connect with this new part and draw it on the page where it wants to be placed.

Step 7: Take some time to look at your parts on the page. Take as long as you need. As you look at your polarized system, what do you notice?

Step 8: You can continue to connect with your polarized system using your drawing to get to know more about each of these parts.

CHAPTER 8

Waterfall

Working with Trauma Expressed in the Body

I was a passenger in a terrible car accident at 19 years old. My boyfriend at the time was driving. He had a green arrow for a left turn when a car came through the intersection and T-boned us on my side of the car. My injuries made it necessary for me to leave my job and college studies to recover. The lasting effects of the accident were severe lower back pain that worsened in times of stress, overwork, and emotional challenge. I sought pain relief from a multitude of medications, physical therapies, yoga, and homeopathic remedies, but nothing provided sustained improvement. I lived with the limitations of excruciating back pain for 26 years before finding true relief.

Two books, *The Mindbody Prescription: Healing the Body, Healing the Pain*, by Dr. John Sarno,[1] and *The MindBody Workbook: A Thirty Day Program of Insight and Awareness for People with Back Pain and Other Disorders*, by Dr. David Schechter,[2] changed the course of how my parts used my body and back pain to communicate with me. Although neither book expressly mentions parts, they both speak of "repressed emotions" such as anger, fear, and unresolved grief and "aspects of personality" such as people pleasing, perfectionism, criticism, controlling, and over-responsibility, all of which are ways parts express in their extreme states.

At the time I read these two books, my life was driven by each of these aspects of personality (parts) and the repressed emotions (parts) of rage, rejection, and shame. I would not allow myself to accept how inadequate I felt as a parent of a child who experienced an unbelievable amount of trauma in the foster care system prior to me adopting her. I believed my education and training as a social worker and my profession as a psychotherapist meant I should be able to help my child recover from their traumatic experiences, and simultaneously I carried the shame of my inability to do so.

My denial of reality, the self-rage at my shortcomings as a parent, the rejection I felt from my child, and the shame of not being the perfect mother of my imaginations expressed in my body by intensifying my back pain.

IFS CONCEPT 1: PROTECTORS AND THE BODY

Parts are both impacted by the body and have impact on the body. They inhibit the body as a way of self-expression to shut us down or rev us up. Each of the three types of parts discussed in earlier chapters uses the body. In the book *Internal Family Systems Therapy, 2nd Edition*, Dr. Richard Schwartz states that parts can create symptoms, maintain, exacerbate, or prolong them.[3] Parts express bodily sensations such as a tightening of the stomach, heat in the torso, or expansiveness in the heart. They may express pain such as a migraine, back pain, or pain in an area of the body that was injured in the past. Parts also assert themselves through illness, either causing illness or using an existing illness to express themselves.

Earlier we learned that protectors are either managers or firefighters. These two types of protectors use the body differently. The preemptive managers need to control vulnerability. They will employ the muscle to keep our attention away from vulnerable parts. A person may experience chronic muscle and/or joint pain to avoid facing feelings of shame. The more exiles in a person's system or the more intense the person's trauma, the more physical ailments managers may use. It is not uncommon for me to have clients who experience multiple manager-related complaints such as tension and migraine headaches, fibromyalgia, jaw pain, fatigue, and/or re-experiencing pain that had previously been controlled. While the person in pain is consumed with diagnoses and treatments, which can take years to prove effective, managers are doing their job of keeping the person's exiles out of awareness.

Reactive firefighters are tasked with suppressing vulnerable feelings once they are experienced. Their behaviors activate fight, flight, freeze, or fawn responses. Their reactions are impulsive and immediate because the threat of vulnerability feels like imminent danger to our firefighters. They may cause heart palpitations to the point of pain, shortness of breath making it hard to breathe, and intense nausea. Additionally, Schwartz explains that "firefighters use physical arousal or desire (e.g., cravings for food, sex, alcohol, drugs, or sleep) to distract from emotions they view as a threat."[4] Firefighters will employ multiple strategies for as long as needed until the emotional pain is completely extinguished.

IFS CONCEPT 2: EXILES AND THE BODY

Exiles use the body to signal their need for help. They have been silenced and hidden away by other parts, caregivers, life experiences, and trauma. They are desperate to receive redemption and tell their story. Because exiles were injured at a young age, some before they were verbal, the pain of their experiences is held in the body. In their quest for redemption and help, they need to be believed. They will use body sensations to get our attention. The ways in which they use the body is directly connected to the abuse, neglect, or terror they experienced. They may communicate through tears, freezing, trembling, smells, and/or the physical pain of their trauma. Exiles hold that if they are heard and believed, they will be redeemed and viewed as worthwhile and lovable.

IFS CONCEPT 3: POLARIZED PARTS AND THE BODY

As we saw in Chapter 7, we are polarized when two parts or groups of parts are in opposition with little access to Self. Each side of the polarization fears the other side taking over, which leads to a power struggle. The most common polarization is that between a manager and a firefighter. The manager's role is to keep us from experiencing painful emotions and vulnerability, while firefighters want to take us out of those feelings when they occur. For example, a person struggling with the decision to stay in an unfulfilling relationship or leave has a polarization. Certain parts have reasons to stay, while opposing parts have reasons to end the relationship. Understandably, there are emotions connected with each side of this decision, and exiled feelings of not being good enough and fear of loneliness.

Managers use the person's body to express anxiety to keep them from feeling hurt, sadness, and unworthiness. While the person remains in the relationship, they may experience an upset stomach, tension headaches, and sustained nervous energy. These experiences are polarized with firefighters who are triggered when the managers' attempts to control these undesirable emotions fail. To douse the unwanted feelings of not being good enough, firefighters use physical arousal of food or alcohol. Due to the polarization, each side will fight to control the person, creating a vicious cycle of physical bodily upset followed by the use of food or alcohol for emotional numbing.

IFS CONCEPT 4: SELF AND THE BODY

In Chapter 4, we learned that Self is the healing agent in the system, and we talked about the eight qualities of Self that the system embodies when parts relax and unblend. There are both similarities and differences between the physical expression of the eight qualities of Self in the body. Let's look at each of the qualities and how they express in the body. This list is not exhaustive. As you read through it, consider how your system embodies the qualities of Self.

Calm is experienced as emotionally and mentally relaxed with a decrease in heart rate, blood pressure, muscle tension, and breathing, creating a feeling of a relaxed mind and body. Clarity is embodied as feeling present, focused, and spacious. Compassion expresses in the body as openheartedness, feeling with another person or part, and an energy toward helping. Confidence is present in the body as a belief in yourself, trusting and accepting yourself, or inner knowing of your abilities. Connectedness embodies ease and comfort with another person or part and feelings of being valued, seen, heard, and validated. Courage is experienced in the body as mental and emotional strength and the ability to overcome fear and act. Creativity expresses as a feeling of being "in flow" or "in the zone." Curiosity embodies openness to learn more and inquisitiveness. It is good practice to notice how Self embodies your system. This will help you to know when Self is leading versus when parts are in the driver's seat.

Case Vignette: A Dose of Nausea

Nausea, retching, and with some clients, vomiting, presents as a powerful and effective firefighter for emergent exile energy. These physical reactions quickly change the focus from the work at hand to what's happening in the body. Sherrie, a white 32-year-old female, was referred to me by her OB/GYN provider for postpartum depression. She had given birth to her third child four months earlier. Her symptoms included depressed mood most days, uncontrollable crying, a desire to "be left alone and sleep," loss of appetite, and shame about not feeling close to her youngest child as she did to her older children. She also experienced pelvic pain with no physical cause found by her medical doctors.

We started our work with the part of her who was having difficulty bonding with her child. This is what she found most upsetting. We spent several sessions building trust and relationship with this part. When she focused on it, she found it in her lower pelvic area and described it as a reddish-orange fiery ball that caused pain. During our session, we had to ask the part to unblend a bit by reducing the intensity of the pain to allow Sherrie to be with it. It took several attempts to get the part to titrate the pain to a level that was tolerable for Sherrie. Once this was accomplished, we learned that the part believed that Sherrie was incapable of taking care of her baby because she was incapable of taking care of herself. Therefore, the part renders her unable to function. She has low energy because she's not eating and she's sleeping a lot, which makes her less available to take care of her child, and her shame about not bonding with her baby is also connected to a fear that she might hurt her child in some way.

It seemed to me that this part did not know Sherrie was an adult. Its view of her appeared juvenile. I asked Sherrie to ask the part, "How old do you think I am?" The part answered, "Three or four." I asked Sherrie to ask the part to look at her to see if it could see that she was a grown-up now. The part still saw her as a child. Next, I had her tell the part her age and share with the part what had happened in her life since she was three or four. Sherrie did this by showing the part highlights of her life like a movie. The part expressed surprise and amazement at her success and ability to take care of herself.

We found out that the part took on its role of protecting Sherrie from things it believed she couldn't handle around age four by making her sad. When asked what caused it to protect in this way, it shared, "Sherrie had a slew of different babysitters and . . ." Mid-sentence of the part's sharing, Sherrie said, "I feel nauseous." She started to sway in her seat, with her head seemingly being rocked on her neck involuntarily. She brought her hand to her mouth, and beads of perspiration were forming on her forehead and top lip. I asked if she was present with this part. She responded, "Barely." I asked if I could speak directly to the part. She nodded. I asked the part, "What are you reacting to?" The part answered, "To all of this—it is too much for her." Curious I asked, "What's too much?" The part responded, "I have to keep her from being hurt." I questioned, "What will hurt her?" The nausea seemed to intensify; Sherrie began sweating more and her stomach started to jerk. I asked the part if it would decrease the nausea. It refused emphatically. Curious about its refusal, I asked, "What are you afraid would happen if you didn't make Sherrie sick and nauseated?" Firmly the part stated, "Sherrie can't handle what happened. I keep that hidden. If I don't stop her . . ." Holding her mouth, Sherrie bolted from her seat and retreated to the bathroom connected to my office. I could hear her retching and spitting. After about a minute, I heard the faucet running. She returned with a wet paper towel, dabbing her forehead and cheeks. She grabbed her purse, said a quick, "I'm sorry," and rushed from my office.

Sherrie's parts used her body in multiple ways. Her manager parts expressed in her body through uncontrollable crying, a loss of appetite, and intense pelvic pain to keep her from experiencing emotional pain and vulnerability. The nausea-causing firefighter took hold of her body with overwhelming nausea, sweating, and retching. This firefighter believed it must take her out to keep experiences from her consciousness. This part continued to show up in future sessions anytime we approached talking about the babysitters. Due to Sherrie's willingness to heal and recover from postpartum depression, we were able to eventually build a Self-to-part relationship with the nausea-causing firefighter and heal the exile under its protection.

Meditation: Waterfall

Waterfall is the eighth meditation co-created with my ancestors. I have parts that communicate with me through my body. I shared one such part, Antsy, in Chapters 5 and 6. At times, I am not even aware of their presence as a part because the physical experience can be overwhelming and even terrifying. This meditation helps me to listen to parts who show up in my body. As with the other meditations they co-created with me, I found it surprising how well my ancestors know me and what I need.

For this meditation, you may want to lie down; however, it can be done sitting up also. This is a parts awareness meditation. Parts can show up in various places in our bodies. This meditation will help you to discover their location in your body and how parts are experienced in your body. If you do not notice a part in a particular location of your body, that's okay; simply allow your awareness to rest on that part of your body.

Close your eyes or soften your gaze.

Adjust your body in whatever way is needed for you to become comfortable.

Bring your awareness to your breath and just breathe.

If it feels right and helps you relax, breathe in for four counts and breathe out for four counts; you can do this several times.

Imagine yourself in the presence of a magnificent waterfall.

You admire its power, grace, and majesty.

You feel the spray of its mist on your face.

Deciding to lie at its feet, you find a soft patch of grass.

With your eyes closed, you begin to calm as the earth cradles you in its arms.

The melody of the waterfall lulls you deeper inside.

Bring your attention to your feet and toes.

Notice how they feel: acknowledge any parts in your feet and toes.

Focus on the part or parts you notice there.

As you focus, what more do you notice?

Move your attention to your legs. Notice how they feel.

Bring your attention to any parts that use your legs; for now, just allow them to be there while you focus on them.

How do you feel toward the parts you notice in your legs?

Move your awareness to your thighs, what do you notice here? Which parts live in your thighs?

Now move to your sit bone. Breathe into this area of your body and see what you notice. Be with whatever you find there.

Bring your attention to your hips. Notice and allow whatever is present.

As you pay more attention to your hips, what do you experience?

Move your awareness around to your stomach or abdomen area. Notice if there are any sensations here, not to change them, just to bring awareness.

How do you feel toward what you're experiencing in your stomach?

Take your attention around to your back. Take your time moving up and down your back noticing any sensations, tightness, or tension.

Travel from your back up to your shoulders. What do you notice here? Are your shoulders up near your ears? Are they relaxed and loose? Whatever you notice is okay.

Move your awareness to your heart. Feel your heartbeat. Is your heart space open, closed, tight, warm, or expansive? Notice and allow what's happening.

Pull your awareness down your arms and into your hands. Notice whatever is present. How do parts use your arms or hands?

Focus on those parts and see what else you notice.

Move your attention to your throat. Notice the air as it passes through your throat. Are there parts that use your throat? Focus on those parts. Be with what you find here.

Pull your awareness up to your face and jaw. Can you feel your expression? Is your jaw tight or relaxed? Just notice.

Now to your eyes, ears, and forehead. Simply be with whatever is present. Notice the parts that show up in your eyes, ears, and forehead. How do you feel toward these parts?

Bring your attention to the top of your head. What do you sense here? As you focus on the top of your head, what more do you notice? Breathe into the top of your head.

Breathe into your whole body, noticing your entire body breathing. Every single part you noticed is breathing.

Bring awareness to how your body feels. From the top of your head back down to your toes, scan each part and notice how your body feels.

If there are parts you need to return to, set an intention with them to do so.

Express gratitude for what your parts shared.

Bring your awareness to your breath and breathe as you re-enter this moment and space.

When it feels right, you can slowly open your eyes.

Exercise 1: Journal Capture

Journal what you would like to capture from this meditation, like a revelation, reflection, or anything significant you want to remember from this experience.

Exercise 2: Waterfall Journal Questions

After you've done the Waterfall meditation and written your quick Journal Capture, take some time to explore more deeply by responding to the following journal prompts.

1. What did you learn about your parts and how they express in your body?
2. How did your body feel at the end of this meditation?
3. What parts were most noticeable, and where were they located in your body?
4. How might knowing how your parts use your body benefit you?
5. Did you experience any familiar sensations in your body? If so, explain.
6. Did you have any new or unfamiliar sensations in your body? If so, explain.
7. Which parts did you commit to return to?

Exercise 3: Naming the Sensations

Circle words below that describe the bodily sensations you experienced during the meditation.

Achy	Cold	Jittery	Queasy	Still
Airy	Constricted	Knotted	Relaxed	Sweaty
Armored	Dense	Light	Restricted	Tearful
Bloated	Dizzy	Nauseous	Rigid	Tender
Blocked	Energized	Numb	Sensitive	Tense
Burning	Expansive	Open	Shaky	Throbbing
Butterflies	Fiery	Pounding	Sharp	Tickly
Clammy	Heavy	Pressure	Sore	Tight
Clenched	Hot	Prickly	Spacious	Tingly
Closed	Itchy	Pulsing	Stiff	Trembling

Add other sensations below:

Exercise 4: Where Parts Live in Your Body

In the space below, sketch a rough outline of your body, then indicate the place of your most dominant parts. Draw a line from that area of the body, and write a word or two to describe the sensations experienced in that area.

CHAPTER 9

The Weary One

Helping Exhausted Parts

When I was traveling with my husband in Mexico a few years ago, I became acutely aware of a part that got frustrated, agitated, irritable, and even angry when life didn't go as planned. The first situation occurred on the ferry to Isla Holbox. I selected seats for us, but he beckoned me to seats further to the front and I moved to his preferred seats. The ferry continued to fill up, with few seats left by the time I put my bags away and settled in next to him. My seat was reclined. I tried to bring the seat back up, and it wouldn't budge. It was broken. My husband reached across me to help. The seat didn't move. I was sitting at an uncomfortable angle, and instantly I felt heat rising in my torso and face. I heard a voice say, "If we had stayed in the seats I chose, I wouldn't be stuck in this broken seat." I looked around the ferry for alternative seats; none were available. I started cussing under my breath and blaming my husband for my discomfort. I said to him in an accusatory tone, "We should have stayed in the other seats." My perceptual field narrowed, and all I could see was him sitting comfortably and me uncomfortable. My body was tense and rigid. My mouth was tight with clenched teeth, my breathing was shallow, and my internal temperature rose. I was hot both physically and emotionally. I was twisting and turning, trying to find a satisfactory way to endure the 30-minute ride. My husband offered me his seat, and my part, in its highly irritable and angry state, growled, "No, I want *this* seat to work."

In the depth of this experience, life outside of me seems not to exist. I am only faintly aware of what is going on around me. However, when a solution is offered, my part needs time to take it in. Slowly, it allows the alternative to creep into its awareness, then gradually becomes aware of life outside of itself.

After 10 minutes of what felt like misery to this part, it requested to change seats with my husband. After another few minutes, I thought, "What just happened? Why did I get so frustrated and angry about being unable to sit upright for 30 minutes? Why didn't I just recline and enjoy the ride? Or accept my husband's initial offer to change seats?" My behavior was baffling to me. The me that didn't understand was another part confused by what it viewed as an overreaction to the situation.

On the same trip, we planned a day of sunning and relaxing at one of our favorite beach clubs. I'd packed our beach bags with sunblock, water, my iPad for reading, a hat, sunglasses, towels—I was ready. The club prepared a delicious ceviche I was looking forward to enjoying. About an hour into our beach time, the part of me that became irritable with the unexpected showed itself again when we got caught in a rainfall that hadn't been in the forecast. Again, I became razor focused, this time about how our day was ruined by the rain. However, this time, unlike with the broken seat, there was a degree of separation from the part, because I was aware while I was in a place of high agitation and anger, life around me continued. People played in the ocean, others sat in beach chairs drinking drinks garnished with colorful umbrellas, and children laughed and ran through the rain. Most of the people around me seemed unfazed by what my part experienced as a joy-stealing event.

The agitation over the ferry seat and the rain caused me to get curious about this part of myself. I wanted to know its story. I realized it was protecting me from something, and I wanted to know the true catalyst for its disproportional reaction to the smallest of unexpected events. By befriending this part and being curious about its story, I learned that it was tired of the automatic response it could not control. It didn't want to overreact, but agitation and anger felt like the only responses available. Although this part didn't know what else to do, it felt terribly exhausted.

IFS CONCEPT: HOPE MERCHANT

Parts become exhausted by the extreme roles they've been forced into. Protectors are highly committed to their jobs, even risking complete exhaustion in protecting the system from the intense emotions of exiles and other parts. In order to support our hard-working protectors, we want to validate their experiences, appreciate how hard they work to keep us safe, and offer opportunity to rest and possibly give up their roles. Self, as what we call the Hope Merchant in IFS, is not offering blind hope to parts. The offering is specific to what parts need to willingly relinquish their role. We can support our exhausted parts and offer them hope that things can improve.

In Chapter 2, we met two types of protectors: proactive protectors (managers) that carry the burden of responsibility and protect through control, and reactive protectors (firefighters) that have the burden of impulsivity and protect by releasing emotional pressure. Both proactive and reactive parts do what they do, believe what they believe, and employ the strategies they do because they don't know any other way. They hold that what they are doing really does keep us safe. Our parts are stuck in a rut of keeping us busy and controlled so we don't experience emotional pain and emptiness, or swiftly taking us out of the pain when it emerges. But protectors aren't good at their jobs. We still endure situations and people in life that activate those unhealed places within. Then why do they do it? Why do they rely on the same tactics over and over?

They do so for three main reasons. First, they aren't aware of any other choice. At some point in their past the strategies they employ made sense, offered relief, and in some ways kept us safe. However, over years and years of use, the tactics have lost whatever effectiveness and usefulness they once possessed. Second, protective parts believe something bad will happen if they stop protecting us. They are the barrier between us and hurt, pain, and even death. From their perspective, not protecting us in the manner they do is not an option. They have sworn to protect us at all costs, and they take their job very seriously. They can't quit. If they do, they fear what will happen to the one they protect. Even when they become weary and ineffective, they won't stop, because every time their strategies offer even a small amount of protection from pain, they are motivated to stay the course. The third and final reason our parts continue to do what doesn't work is that they have no awareness of Self, no relationship with

Self, or no trust in Self. Remember, these parts took on their job responsibilities in most cases when we were very young. They may have felt alone and had to figure things out for themselves. With this mindset, they came up with the best solution they could at the time. They did so then and continue to do so now without connection with Self. If parts knew they no longer had to carry the burden of being responsible for our safety—if they knew there's a resource within that can help—most would gladly consider, if not readily accept, the assistance. That said, parts may have learned through their lived experience not to trust Self. Expressing qualities of Self such as confidence, courage, and/or curiosity could have resulted in belittling, humiliation, abuse, or neglect. Since Self-energy was countered with harshness, parts believe Self is unsafe and not trustworthy.

The antidote to the exhaustion parts feel is hope of improvement. Hope opens them to the possibility of another way of being. The way to offer them hope is through a series of questions, or Hope Merchant steps, which I'll share here as outlined by IFS senior lead trainer Pamela Krause.[1]

The job of these tired parts is to ensure that we are never hurt the way we were when they took on their roles. To help them, we must first know what their greatest fear is, then address it. Therefore, after the part is in relationship with Self through befriending and getting to know the part's story, we can ask the part, "What are you afraid would happen if you didn't (fill in what the part does to protect)?" The answer points to fear of the exiled part being hurt or feeling the pain of being unlovable, worthless, or not good enough and/or overwhelming the system with its intense emotions. If the first answer given does not reflect the exile's pain, ask the protector what it is afraid would happen if (the answer they gave) happens. For example, if the protector initially answered, "There would be no one to protect the young one." Then ask, "What are you afraid would happen if there was no one to protect the young one?" Continue this line of questioning until you get an answer that reflects the exiled part's pain like, "I'm afraid the young one will feel ashamed and disgusting." Once we know the fear that motivates the protector to push through exhaustion, we offer to address it: "What if I could go to the one who feels ashamed and disgusting and heal it so you wouldn't have to feel so exhausted? Would you be interested?"

The most important point when asking the Hope Merchant questions is using the part's exact words. This deepens connection and trust. The part feels heard. Since the goal is to offer hope for the part's specific concerns, precise wording matters. Besides, if different words are used that miss the intended meaning, this may upset the part and cause it to feel misunderstood, and we may miss the opportunity to instill the hope that the part's situation can improve.

Pricklee

At the start of this chapter, I described an experience with one of my parts who becomes irritable, upset, and angry when life doesn't go as it expected. Now I want to share with you what I learned when I got curious about why I responded as I did to the broken seat and the unanticipated rain shower. I have discovered in my personal work and my work with clients that the Self qualities of curiosity and compassion are effective ways to come into relationship with our parts. The very act of being curious allows for some separation between Self and the part. It is only with this separation that we can begin to connect with the part. If you remember my responses and actions on the ferry, I was blended with the part who was irritated; that part was in the driver's seat. If a part is in the seat of consciousness, we cannot be with it. I often say, "I can't be with a part when I'm being the part." My awareness of being blended came when another part questioned why I behaved the way I did. This part had a critical tone and didn't like the part who was irritable. The curiosity of Self came forth, and I asked the part who expressed dislike for the first part to step back and allow me to be with the part that felt irritable and angry. That part stepped back. I closed my eyes to see what I noticed inside. I felt tightness and heat in my jaw and a feeling of exasperation. The feelings were at a level that allowed separation. Self let the part know that it was curious about the part's experiences and wanted to get to know it. Self sent the energy of curiosity to the tightness in my jaw and sat with the experience. The clenching loosened. Self thanked the part for releasing some of the tension. The feeling of exasperation decreased a bit too.

At that point, curiosity increases. Self sends the part the energy of curiosity. Self wants to know and understand the experiences of this part and wants it to feel Self's desire to get to know it better. Self asks, "What do you want me to know about you?" The part quickly responds, "My name is Prickly, spelled P-R-I-C-K-L-E-E, never L-Y." The way she emphasizes *never* gives Self the sense that the distinction is very important. "Got it, Pricklee, L-E-E. What about life not going as you expect causes you to feel irritable?"

She responds, "I like to know how things are going to turn out. I don't like it when the unpredictable happens.

I want to be prepared for bad things." Self is now curious about the connection between the unexpected and bad things happening. Self says, "It makes sense to want to be prepared in case something bad happens. Have unexpected bad things happened to you?" Pricklee emphatically says, "Yes, they have." "I'm interested to know more about that," Self says in an inquiring tone. Pricklee totally relaxes her (my) jaw as she projects her experiences as a movie playing before my eyes.

The first scene is of me at about age nine traveling on a plane with my younger sister and brother to visit our paternal grandparents in Louisiana for the summer. I see a stewardess attending to us with food and beverages. I feel the excitement and fear in my physical body that my younger self felt during the flight. I see myself coloring happily in a book about planes and travel. I'm then shown a scene of the stewardess pinning golden wings on the lapel of my blouse. I sense that my younger self felt so special.

The next scene is a montage of various activities and experiences while visiting that summer. My two youngest aunts were home from college. They were both in their early 20s at the time. I saw flashes of them taking me to the public swimming pool, to Grambling State University where they both attended college, to the local grocery store to get candy, chips, and soda. Next, I saw myself eating figs off the tree in the yard until my stomach hurt. My grandmother teaching me to sew on her black-and-gold Singer sewing machine with the large circle thing that made the needle go up and down. We were making dresses for my Barbie dolls. Pricklee even played a scene of me getting into mischief with my cousins throwing rocks at the glass-paned roof of an abandoned plant nursery. In these scenes, I felt Pricklee's light expansiveness of joy and playfulness.

The final scenes begin with my nine-year-old self going to the mailbox at the road to collect the mail, which was one of her daily chores. She recognized the bold, strong box lettering on one of the envelopes as her father's printing. The next thing she noticed literally took her breath away. The return address was not her home address in Marina del Rey, California, but an unknown address in Inglewood, California. She was confused and didn't understand why her father would have a new, different address. I could feel the strain of her trying to make sense of what she read. Wondering if this was the address of the apartment building he and Mom owned. But why would he put that address on the envelope? Although she didn't understand, she felt that something was very wrong. She ran into the house with tears on her face, demanding that her grandmother tell her why her father had a new address. Her grandmother said she didn't know, but my younger self knew she was lying. Pricklee next showed a scene of me asking my grandmother what the letter said. My grandmother refused, saying, "It's not mine to tell." I felt nine-year-old Tamala's outrage at the truth being withheld and her terror of the unknown.

Gone were the carefree days of cheerfully swimming, sewing, and eating handpicked figs. She was consumed with wanting to know the contents of her father's letter and the significance of the return address. No one would tell her what was going on back home. Everyone claimed to have no idea. She begged and cried to go home. She believed she could fix whatever was wrong if she could return. She was only told she would talk to her parents soon. When she finally spoke with her parents by phone, they just told her to enjoy her summer and they would talk about it when she got home. Which was all she wanted to do, go home. The phone call left her anxious and fearful.

The next thing my nine-year-old self communicates comes in the feeling of having the wind knocked out of her. She felt blindsided and abandoned. There was no one to help her manage her overwhelming feelings. Her heart physically hurt, and she didn't understand the agonizing pain. Her tears began to flow from my eyes. I felt the intensity of her suffering and desperation. She didn't want to face what she knew. She wanted someone to tell her that her fears were not true, but their secrecy only confirmed them. She had sensed high tension between her parents before she left for Louisiana. She knew her mother was unhappy. In her mind, her parents' fighting, not speaking to each other, her mother's unhappiness, and her father's new address meant her parents were getting a divorce and her father had moved out. Self continued to offer my younger self the sincerest compassion for her experience and the shock of it. Pricklee went on to share that she made a promise to never allow anything to catch her unaware again. It hurt much too much. Her life would be predictable and knowable to protect her heart from this unbearable pain.

From connecting with my parts from Self-energy, I became aware that Pricklee is the part of me who becomes irritable, and she exiled nine-year-old Tamala as a way to make life predictable and protect her from the pain of being blindsided again. Pricklee's carefree, fun-loving nature was eclipsed by the responsibility to protect the system from experiencing the pain of abandonment and being alone with big, scary emotions.

After sharing how hard she's been working to protect young Tamala, Pricklee expresses how exhausted she is. She admits feeling stressed out trying to control everything and predict every outcome. She is constantly on high alert, looking for what could go wrong. Pricklee is only calm when things go as planned, and any deviation from the plan causes anxiety, annoyance, or anger. Self asks her, "What are you afraid would happen if you didn't control everything and predict every outcome?" She answers, "The brokenhearted pain will come and steal our joy forever, and we'll never be carefree again." Self feels deep compassion for the dedication of this part to protect and offers, "What if I could go to the one who feels the brokenhearted pain and heal it so you wouldn't have to feel so exhausted. Would you be interested?" With relief and slight doubt, she asks, "You can do that?" In reassurance Self answers, "Yes, with your permission I can."

It's not surprising that our parts are exhausted. Many have been protecting us since we were young. The irony of their tiring work is that the vulnerable parts they protect are not changed or healed by their efforts. Our young parts continue to feel and express their pain, unworthiness, and/or shame. The experiences Pricklee is trying to protect me from, joylessness and not being carefree, are exactly what she creates when things don't go as she expects. The joy of arriving to Isla Holbox by ferry for the first time was overshadowed by Pricklee's irritation and anger. Enjoying the beach in a rain shower was not the day Pricklee had planned, therefore her ire canceled what could have been a carefree, fun experience. Our protectors' intention is to protect us, but their strategies fall short.

It's important to understand that our parts are forced into extreme protective roles based on their experiences.

Pricklee wasn't born irritable and needing to protect. In her natural state, she was fun-loving, curious, expressive, and adventurous. She both absorbed the life occurring around her and became a part of it. Her firsthand experience of being left alone with her emotions and unanswered questions led her to feel unsafe and increased her need for certainty and predictability. Today, when she doesn't get those, she escalates to irritability and anger in fear that the nine-year-old she protects will be harmed again.

Meditation: The Weary One

The Weary One meditation is the fourth meditation given me by my ancestors. This meditation came at a time when many of my parts were tired and overworked. I was seeing psychotherapy clients full-time while building an IFS consultation practice for therapists and working toward becoming an IFS lead trainer. Not to mention all the other activities of life.

This meditation supports parts that are exhausted in their role. It's a chance to connect and learn the part's story, its job, and why it's exhausted. This meditation offers hope to a weary part that life can be different, and it doesn't have to work so hard.

Relax and find a comfortable position to help your body settle.
Close your eyes if that feels right.
As you go inside, notice your breath.
Is it shallow and short or deep and long?
As you notice, see if you can lengthen and deepen each breath.

Find a part that is weary, exhausted, or tired.
Notice where this part shows up in or near your body.
Focus on how tired this part is.
As you focus, what do you notice?

Choose a place to go with the part to relax and learn more.

This could be a place in nature, you could cuddle near a fire, or take a relaxing walk; you can go anywhere you'd like to go.

Encourage the part to rest in your presence if it can.

You can talk if the part wants to, but it is not necessary; you can just be with the part for a while.

If the part wants to talk, ask the part about its weariness.

What causes the exhaustion?

How long has it been doing what causes the tiredness?

Why did the part take on this role?

Listen and offer compassion for how hard this part is working.

Ask the part, "What are you afraid would happen if you stopped doing this role?"

Address the fears the part shares with you.

Offer hope by saying, "What if I could heal the vulnerable one you protect so you won't be so weary. Would you be interested?"

Be with the part as it expresses its concerns or interests.

If it has concerns, address them.

If the part is interested, let it know that all it has to do is give permission and step back.

Express gratitude for how hard this part is working and set an intention with the part.

Bring your awareness to your breath, and when it feels right, reenter this moment and space. Slowly open your eyes when you're ready.

Exercise 1: Journal Capture

Journal what you would like to capture from this meditation, like a revelation, reflection, or anything significant you want to remember from this experience.

Exercise 2: The Weary One Journal Questions

After you've done the Weary One meditation and written your quick Journal Capture, take some time to explore more deeply by responding to the following journal prompts.

1. What did you notice when you first connected with your part?
2. Where and how does the weary part show up in your body?
3. If there is an image connected with this part, draw it here or in your journal. Does this part have a name? If so, write it here ______________________________ or in your journal.
4. As you got to know the part, what did you learn about its weariness?
   a. Causes of the exhaustion
   b. How long it's been doing its job
   c. Why it took on its job
5. How did you feel toward this part after hearing its story?
6. What did you discover about this part's fears about releasing its role?
7. Did you notice a change in the part's weariness during the meditation? If so, what did you notice?
8. Who is the vulnerable one this part protects?
9. Is the part willing to step back? If not, why not?
10. What intentions did you set with this part?
11. Journal anything else about this experience you want to capture.

Exercise 3: Hope Merchant Practice

In this practice, you will get to know a protector and offer hope for change.

Step 1: Identify a part you want to get to know.

Step 2: Notice where/how the part expresses in/around your body.

Step 3: Focus on how you experience this part.

Step 4: How do you feel toward this part? If it's one of the eight Cs, send that energy to the part. If not one of the eight Cs, ask the new part to step back. If the part does not step back, spend time getting to know that part; address its fears. If and when it is willing to step back, move to Step 5.

Step 5: Notice how the part responds to your Self-energy. If there is a positive shift, acknowledge it and offer appreciation.

Step 6: Continue to extend Self-energy (one or more of the eight Cs).

Step 7: Create a Self-to-part relationship by asking the part what it wants you to know about itself.

Step 8: Validate the part's experiences.

Step 9: Continue to extend Self-energy (one or more of the eight Cs).

Step 10: Ask the part to share more of its story with you (it may use images, bodily sensations, words, etc.).

Step 11: Find out what the part is afraid of by asking, "What are you afraid would happen if you didn't ________________? (Use the part's exact words for what's it's doing to protect you.)

Step 12: Offer hope by saying, "What if I could go to the one who feels ____________________________________ (use the part's exact words) and heal it. Would you be interested?"

Step 13: Let the part know it does not have to stop doing its job; it only needs to step back.

CHAPTER 10

Elemental Healing

Unburdening and Healing Your Parts

In the last chapter, we met my part Pricklee and discovered that she protected a nine-year-old part of me who experienced feelings of abandonment and being alone after the adults in her life hid the truth about her parents' marriage from her. She knew in her gut that they were separated and getting divorced. She needed her grandmother, aunts, or parents to confirm what she already knew to be true. Because no one did, young Tamala was left to manage her emotions and started to doubt her own sense of reality. Everyone wanted her to continue with her summer as if nothing devastating was occurring in her life, but she couldn't pretend and deny the real pain of her broken heart. Pricklee took over to protect this vulnerable, hurt, lonely part of me. She exiled the pained one and became hypervigilant in her need for predictability. When she didn't get it, she became anxious, irritated, and angry for fear that I would experience the abandonment, heartbreak, and loneliness of the one she protects by keeping her exiled.

Although Pricklee expressed skepticism about my ability to heal young Tamala, she allowed access. When I closed my eyes and went inside, I entered a space where I was able to see and even touch young Tamala. I saw my younger self crouching in a corner with her back to me. She was silently crying several feet away. My compassion for her was palpable. I wanted to go scoop her up and hold her, and I wanted to honor her space at the same time. I sent the energy of compassion I felt in her direction. It took several minutes for her to look over her shoulder toward me with interest. I smiled. I asked if I could come closer. She answered by scooting close enough for us to touch, although we didn't. I continued to energetically share the energy of curiosity and compassion with her. This piqued her curiosity because she asked, "Who are you?" I told her, "I'm you all grown up." My eyes welled up with her tears as she moved beside me close enough for our legs to touch. I felt her sadness and relief. She looked into my eyes and said, half a statement and half a question, "You're me and I'm you?" I nodded. Then she asked, "What took you so long?" I simply answered, "I'm here for you now and want to get to know you." I felt a rush of her deep sadness. But even with feeling her sadness, I was able to remain present with her continuing to extend my Self-energy of genuine curiosity.

Tearfully, she said, "No one loves me enough to tell me the truth." She went on to share how the adults in her life broke her heart. They made it so she could not trust herself any longer. She knew that things were not okay at home when she saw the return address on the letter from her father to her grandmother. But for some reason, the adults tried to convince her that everything was fine. She didn't understand why they didn't love her enough to tell her the truth. She was further confused by her grandmother's lies because she herself was always told to tell the truth. She came to believe that she wasn't worth being told the truth. When she shared the intense agony of her worthlessness, her body crumpled, and a torrent of tears fell from my eyes. I felt profoundly connected to her in this moment, and my compassion intensified. I reached for her, and she snuggled to the curves of my body, allowing me to comfort her. I let her know I could hold every pain she experienced and that she was no longer alone. I felt her body relax, and her tears began to subside. I softly asked, "Is there more you want to share?" She nodded and asserted, "I trusted myself before this happened. I knew things, and I didn't know how I knew them. I trusted what I knew because it felt right. But this made me distrust myself. I lost my gift." I supportively offered, "Are you ready to release your burdens from that experience?" She nodded eagerly.

IFS CONCEPT 1: BURDENS REVISITED

Burdens are created out of our woundedness. Neglect, abuse, rejection, lack of attunement to our needs, boundary violations, attachment injuries—all these can result in wounding. Our parts get the message that something is wrong with them. From these experiences parts become burdened with extreme beliefs about themselves, others, and the world. These burdens become a part of them, but they are not who the part naturally is. In most cases, parts are not created burdened; rather, their essential nature becomes obscured by the burdens.

In the example of my nine-year-old exiled part, she was burdened with feelings of worthlessness, abandonment, aloneness, and the physical pain of brokenheartedness. These burdens covered up her natural ability to trust her intuition, planting the seeds of self-doubt. Healing involves helping our exiled parts release their burdens.

IFS CONCEPT 2: WITNESSING REVISITED

The process of healing an exile is called unburdening, and the key step in it is witnessing. The goal of witnessing is for the exiled part to feel heard and understood by Self. It is important to slow down and not rush the process of getting to know exiled parts. When a protector gives permission and access to get to know an exile, we want to notice how we experience the exile when we go inside. The part may express itself as a sensation in the body such as tightness, numbness, chills, or any other sensation. It may allow us to experience its emotions like terror, sadness, or hopelessness. It may even present in physical form. Sometimes our exiled parts show up as a younger version of ourselves.

It is not uncommon for exile parts to blend with us. They have been hidden away for a long time and are needy of attention. As we learned earlier, we cannot form a relationship with a part when it is blended with us. We want to ask the exile part early on not to blend with us. If it does, we can ask the part to unblend. However, it is easier and more efficient to ask a part not to blend in the beginning than it is to ask it to unblend later.

Regardless of the way exile parts first express themselves, we need to build a trusting relationship with them. We accomplish this by extending Self-energy to the part. Upon first meeting our exiled parts, we may feel compassion for what they have gone through. We also may feel connected to them and curious about their experiences. If they are scared or upset, we may feel calm toward them. Whatever C-word we feel, we let them feel it too, energetically. The part may not notice us or may feel hostile toward us; we want to continue to send our Self-energy to it until it shifts in some way. Experiencing our compassion, curiosity, confidence, etc., will help the exile calm and notice us. It may even get curious about who we are and why we are present. From this awareness, we can begin to build a relationship with the exile. Remember these are usually young parts and we want to engage them as such. Think about how you would interact with a young child. We may soften or lower our voice, speak slower, get on the child's level, offer a physical connection if the child is open to it. We would use these same methods to build trust with our exiled parts.

After there is trust between you and your exile, you can move into witnessing. Witnessing is the process by which we learn the exiled part's story. How was it wounded? The pains and burdens it carries. We let the part know that we want to know about it. You can ask, "What is it you'd like me to know about you?" Listen and be with the part however it needs you to be with it. The beauty of Self is it is intuitive. When we are Self-led, we don't have to know at a thinking level what to do to support our exiled parts. The part may use various avenues to share its story. Sometimes parts share with images or a movie of what happened to them. There may be multiple scenes they want to share with you. They could use words, sensations, emotions, memories as ways to let you know about their experiences. The process of witnessing takes as long as it needs for the part to share everything it wants to share with you. The most important part of this process is that the part feels heard and validated by you. Up until this point, the part hasn't had the opportunity to share its story with a compassionate listener who doesn't judge it.

In the witnessing, other parts may get overwhelmed, concerned, or fearful about what the exile is sharing. If this happens, ask those parts to step back to allow you to continue to witness the exile's experience. If the parts are unwilling to step back, take time to hear their concerns or fears. Let them know that you want to help them by helping the exile to heal. Their fears are warranted given their experiences too. Listen to them for as long as it takes to address their fears and return to the exile. The witnessing process is complete when the exile feels understood by Self. When the part expresses that it does feel heard and understood and has nothing more to share, we can move forward.

IFS CONCEPT 3: THE DO-OVER

Sometimes as part of the healing process, exiles need for something to occur in the scenes from the past that didn't initially happen; however, this may not be needed for all exiles. As an example, they need support they didn't receive, or they need to say something or do something that they couldn't do or say at the time. As part of the witnessing process, you can offer your exile a do-over.

A do-over is an emotionally corrective experience. The exile has an opportunity to get their needs met in the manner that eluded them originally. This is accomplished by asking your exile, "What do you need to happen that didn't?" or "How did you need someone to be with you back then?" Whatever your part requests of you, provide it for them. They may ask you to stand up to a bully or listen to and hold them or help them with big emotions they don't understand and can't regulate.

When I offered a do-over to my nine-year-old part, she needed three things to happen differently. First, she needed to be told the truth about her dad's address change and her parents' separation. Second, she needed this truth to validate her intuition. Lastly, she needed the adults to help her with the pain of her parents' separation, let her experience her emotions fully, and not expect her to pretend everything was all right.

IFS CONCEPT 4: RETRIEVAL

Some exiled parts may be stuck or frozen in a past trauma scene. The part reexperiences their wounding, unable to extricate themselves from perpetual pain. When this is true, retrieval is necessary. Again, this is a step not necessary for every exile. Retrieval is offering the part a choice to leave the trauma scene for a safe place. Parts often choose to come to the present with Self. They may also choose to go to a place that was safe in the past, such as a grandparent's home. They can also go to an imaginary place or fun location like an amusement park or beach. It is completely the part's choice. Self can escort the part to any place of its choosing. To begin the retrieval, Self simply needs to ask the part, "Are you ready to leave that time and place to come to the present with me or to any other safe place, imaginary or real?" If the part does not want to leave the past, inquire why it doesn't want to leave. Sometimes more witnessing is required. The part may not want to leave until it tells more of its story. Or something more may need to happen in the past. It may be concerned about who it is leaving behind, such as younger siblings who were also impacted by the trauma experience. If this is true, invite the part to bring their siblings with them. Once the part is in a safe place, the unburdening can begin.

Retrieval was not necessary with my nine-year-old exile. She did not feel frozen in the past; she had the ability to leave on her own. When she sat next to me while building trust, she was no longer in the past and felt safe with me in the present.

IFS CONCEPT 5: UNBURDENING

Unburdening is the process by which the exile releases their burdens. This step is crucial to the healing of the exile. Burdens include extreme beliefs like "I am worthless" or "I am unlovable"; extreme bodily sensations such as reexperiencing the effects of neglect or abuse; and intense feelings and emotions such as shame. Because burdens are often held in the body, this is where we begin with the unburdening process. Self asks the part where it notices the burden in or around its body. Once the part connects with where the burden is, Self asks the part if it is ready to release the burden. Parts are usually eager to let go of their burdens. However, sometimes they are reluctant. In this case, the part may need additional time in witnessing, or Self can explore the fears the part has about releasing the burden. If the exile is ready to release their burdens, the Self can offer the release of the burdens to one of the elements: fire, water, air, earth, or any other way the part would like to release the burdens. It is important for the part to release the burden from where it's located in the body. Self supports the part in releasing the burden by helping it set up the release to the elements or simply by being present during the unburdening. The burdens can be released together at one time or individually. It's crucial to check with the exile to see if there's more to unburden after each burden is released. Similar to witnessing, it is the part that determines when the unburdening is complete.

When my nine-year-old exile expressed enthusiasm about the prospect of releasing her burdens, I asked her,

"What are the burdens you're ready to let go of?" She didn't answer in words; instead, I had a felt sense of her desire to release feelings of unworthiness, aloneness, and abandonment, the belief that she was unlovable because if she was lovable people would have told her the truth, difficulty managing her emotions, chest pains of a broken heart, and disconnection from her intuition. Next, I asked her where she noticed these burdens in or around her body. In response, I felt heat in my solar plexus. I then inquired about how she would like to release her burdens by saying, "You can release them to fire, air, water, earth, or any other way you would like to release them." She said she wanted to release them to water at the beach and watch them float away. Next, we were at the water's edge on a beach, and I asked her to remove the burdens from her solar plexus and release them to the water. As she did this, I encouraged her to make sure she got it all. It took several minutes for her to empty the many burdens into the surf. We watched the waves take the burdens out toward the horizon until they disappeared.

IFS CONCEPT 6: INVITATION

When parts are burdened, they do not have access to their natural gifts. The invitation is a way to connect with their essential essence and positive qualities they need moving forward. The release of their burdens opens space for these qualities to exist within. Self encourages the newly unburdened part to invite in qualities it believes it will need in the future and to access their essential qualities that were obscured by the burdens they carried. It is quite common for parts to choose qualities of Self. Just as it was crucial that the part physically released the burdens from its body, it is equally important for the part to embody the qualities it selects. The part can use the elements—fire, air, water, and earth—or any other ritual to assist with embodiment of the qualities. Self is present with the part to offer support.

When Self asked my nine-year-old part what essential qualities she wanted to embody, she asserted, "Intuition!" She went on to explain that the experience of being lied to by the adults she trusted severed her connection with her sense of knowing. When asked if there were any other qualities she wished to embody, she tearfully answered, "My intuition was my greatest gift, and not trusting it was my greatest loss. If I can get it back, I will be whole. It is all I need." When asked how she would like to embody intuition, she took a deep inhale and said, "With my breath," and proceeded to breathe deeply. With each breath, intuition came into my body as well as hers and coursed through our bloodstreams, infusing every inch of our bodies with its energy, with most of it accumulating in our hearts. Self asked my younger self to check her body and see what she noticed. She said, "I feel calm and connected."

Case Vignette: Retrieving an Exile

The case vignette that follows highlights the retrieval step of the healing process. Again, this step is not always needed. However, when an exiled part is stuck in the past or in a trauma scene, it is used to get them to a place safe enough to continue the healing work.

May is Caucasian, in her early 50s, and came to therapy after her decades-long difficulties with sexual penetration were determined to have no physical origins. In her intake she disclosed that she and her younger sister were sexually trafficked by her mother's boyfriend. As a teacher with summers off, he offered to babysit them to help her mother save on childcare costs. During the summers when May was eight and nine, he sold her and her sister to grown men for sex.

In this session, May established a Self-to-part relationship with an exiled part she called Ragdoll, who seemed to trust May's Self. I asked May to ask Ragdoll if there's anything she wants May to know about her.

"Ragdoll, I'm here and you're safe. What do you want to tell me about you?"

May, in Ragdoll's voice, says, "STOP, no, stop, don't! They're hurting me. I don't want to. Nooooo!" May's body trembles, and tears flow as she flails her arms at an unseen assailant.

"May, are you there with Ragdoll?"

"Yes, I am. I'm letting her know I'm here."

"Does she know you're there?"

May lets out a muffled scream as if her mouth is covered.

"See if Ragdoll can pull herself away from you a bit," I suggest, realizing Ragdoll is blending somewhat with May.

"Ragdoll, I want to be with you. Can you give me a little space?"

Ragdoll responds by shaking her head, still fighting, and says, "Make them stop touching me."

"May, ask Ragdoll if there's someplace safe she wants to go. Let her know she can leave there," I share with hopes of getting Ragdoll out of the trauma scene.

"Ragdoll, you don't have to be there," May says. You can go someplace safe, anyplace. You can come here with me. Where would you like to go?"

In a whisper, as if to keep others from hearing her, she says to May, "I want to be with you."

"Great," I say. "May, can you help her to come be with you?"

May is quiet being with Ragdoll internally, then says, "She says she wants to leave but can't."

"Are you curious why she doesn't want to leave May?"

"Yes."

"Then ask her why she can't leave."

May gets quiet again and quickly responds, "Her little sister is in the other room and she won't leave without her."

"Okay, May, that makes sense. You may have to go into the scene with Ragdoll to help get her sister. Check if she's open to that."

"She is." After a moment of silence, May says, "I've got Ragdoll and she's taking me to her sister." Tears are streaming down May's face as she reports what's happening. "I've got her sister now. They're both safely with me, curled up in my lap. I'm letting them know they're safe with me and never have to go back there."

"Good. Hold them like that for as long as they need it."

After Ragdoll and her sister were retrieved, Ragdoll felt safe enough to share her experiences through witnessing. She was incapable of doing so while she was stuck in the scene of her trauma, actively experiencing the abuse. Just as in the external world, safety has to be addressed from the inside first.

Meditation: Elemental Healing

The Elemental Healing meditation is the second given to me by my ancestors.

This meditation allows you to meet an Ancestor Guide and, with their support, release a belief, behavior, thought, or feeling that no longer serves you.

Close your eyes or soften your gaze.

Bring your awareness to your breath and just breathe.

As you go inside, notice how your breath travels through your body, nourishing every place it touches.

Envision yourself near a body of water at sunrise.

It could be a beach, river, lake, stream, or any other body of water.

Notice that the sun is just over the horizon, and you marvel at the colors dancing in the sky.

You start walking the shore, and in the distance you see a robed figure walking toward you.

A calmness embraces you as you get closer and see a serene smile on the other's face.

You recognize them as a wise and benevolent Ancestor Guide.

The Ancestor Guide says, "I've come to help you release something that no longer serves you."

They go on to say, "I'd like you to consider a belief, behavior, feeling, or thought that has outgrown its usefulness."

Once you identify what no longer serves you, notice where you find it in or around your body.

Place your attention on what you notice there.

The Ancestor Guide tells you absent this belief, behavior, feeling, or thought you can be your true Self. All you have to do is release it.

The Ancestor Guide walks with you to the water's edge and says, "You can release it to this body of water. The Ancestor Guide digs a hole in the earth and says, "You can bury it in the Earth's belly." A bonfire appears, and the Ancestor Guide says, "You can allow the fire to consume it." The Ancestor Guide then waves their arms and says, "You can release it on the wind." They turn to you and ask, "In which way would you like to be free of what no longer serves you?"

If you are not able to release it, let the Ancestor Guide know what you are afraid would happen if you released it. It is okay to spend time getting to know the parts of you that are afraid with the support of your Ancestor Guide.

If you are ready to release it, the Ancestor Guide helps you in the way of your choosing.

After the release, take time to share with your Ancestor Guide what it feels like to release what is no longer useful.

Take another minute to finish with your Ancestor Guide, knowing you can connect again whenever you like.

When it feels right, bring your awareness to your breath and just breathe as you re-enter this moment and space.

Slowly open your eyes when you are ready.

Exercise 1: Journal Capture

Journal what you would like to capture from this meditation, like a revelation, reflection, or anything significant you want to remember from this experience.

Exercise 2: Elemental Healing Journal Questions

After you've done the Elemental Healing meditation and written your quick Journal Capture, take some time to explore more deeply by responding to the following journal prompts.

1. What did you identify that no longer serves you?
2. What are the reasons it no longer serves you?
3. Were you able to release it?
4. How might your life and relationships be impacted by this release?
5. If you were not able to release it, why not?
6. What were the fears you discovered?
7. How might you address the fears?
8. When you spent time with your Ancestor Guide, what did you learn?

CHAPTER 11

Cabin with the Ancestor

Healing Family and Cultural Legacy Burdens

Playa del Rey Elementary School, fifth grade, Mr. Dempsey's class. I sit motionless as he places the graded science test face down on my desk. I'm too scared to turn it over and look at my score. I rationalize that I did my best. I studied hard. I reviewed my flashcards daily, even up to moments before taking the exam. I re-read the chapters covered and even did some of the experiments at home. But even with all the preparation, I had a sinking feeling that the grade at the top of this test would not be my customary A. It was important to me to get an A, and if it was a 100% A, that was better. A perfect score was my aim in school and everything else I did. I slowly turned the paper over to discover a large, red C.

Fear gripped me as I studied the curve of the first C of my young academic career. Frozen, I thought, "How can I go home with such a disappointing grade?" I even considered how I could change the C to a B. Staring at the arch of the C, I quickly realized I could not alter it to a believable B. C is for *crushed*, how I felt being less than perfect.

I grew up with a father who sought perfection at all costs. It was much more important to him how things looked than how they were. He modeled external perfection through his speech, dress, mannerisms, and his strong expression of right and wrong. We had to live in the right neighborhood, go to the right schools, join the right clubs. My siblings and I had to speak articulately, dress impeccably, possess manners beyond reproach, and demonstrate high intellect. But I was a tomboy who didn't like bows and dresses, at times chewed with my mouth open, and said "ain't" often. However, I was smart, and although my dad corrected and criticized me for the behaviors that were less than perfect, he praised me for my intellect. I worked hard to fit into his vision of me. I wanted to meet his expectations. I came to equate my dad's love with the need to be perfect. Scared to present my science test to him, I walked the mile from school to home in record slow time.

When I arrived, I found my dad in the living room waiting. He jokingly asked, "Let me see that A." I cringed at the thought of showing him my test. I stammered in a low voice, "I-I-I didn't get an A." Disappointed, he replied, "Getting a B isn't bad. Let me see it." I was rooted in place as tears traced my face. When I was able to uproot myself, I slowly moved toward the couch where he sat and handed him the test. I could feel my insides shaking as I nervously waited for his response. The disdain on his face is forever imprinted in my memory, as well as the sting of his words: "I don't have any average children." In six words, my dad disowned me. I shut down in the shame that he no longer wanted me. I disconnected from the conversation, and only certain words penetrated my consciousness. I heard "unacceptable, unbelievable, disappointed." Next, he pointed firmly to the stairs, demanding that I go to my room.

I bawled on my bed inconsolably. When there were no more tears to cry, I started thinking of ways to prove to my dad that I was perfect and deserving. I imagined getting a perfect score on every test I would ever take. I promised myself that I would practice saying "isn't" instead of "ain't." I would walk with perfect posture. I would be the model of perfection. The little girl my father could never disown again.

My plans of excellence were interrupted by light knocking on my door. I heard my mom say, "Tamala, can I come in?" as she slowly opened the door. My mom told me that she had spoken with my dad about my science test. When I heard this, I started to sob again. She held me and asked, "Did you do your best?" I answered that I did. She held my face and looked directly into my eyes and said, "Tamala, your best is always good enough. You can't do better than your best, and sometimes your best is going to be a C, and that's okay." It felt good to hear this. But I was split; part of me felt redeemed, while another part could not let go of the need to pursue perfection.

IFS CONCEPT 1: PERSONAL VS. LEGACY BURDENS

As defined earlier, burdens are the extreme thoughts, beliefs, behaviors, emotions, and impulses parts take on because of trauma. Parts are not their burdens. The burden is how they have learned to cope with what happened to them. Parts are highly motivated to protect themselves, other parts, and the person from being hurt again. The pattern of protection becomes so entrenched that parts do not know any other way to operate within the system. A burden is a protective strategy that has outlived its usefulness.

There are two types of burdens: personal and legacy. Personal burdens, as we discussed in Chapter 10, are burdens created through our direct lived experiences, while legacy burdens are defined as burdens inherited or passed down from the family, ethnic group, or culture. With legacy burdens the content of the original trauma is lost over time; however, the shame, lack of safety, and feelings of uncertainty, judgment, and being devalued are what's passed down through the family lineage.[1] Following are two case vignettes showing how the burden of anxiety can develop as a personal or legacy burden.

Case Vignette 1: Anxiety as a Personal Burden

Shyla's family immigrated to the United States from India when she was four years old. Shyla was the oldest of three girls, with the youngest child having special medical needs that required a lot of her mother's attention. Shyla's father worked full-time as a university professor. She entered school not speaking English, which caused her a great deal of anxiety. For the first year of kindergarten, she rarely knew what was happening in her classroom. Her anxiety increased with the teasing she received from other children because she looked, dressed, and spoke differently. Eventually, Shyla internalized the teasing and her lack of understanding English as her being stupid and not good enough. Her nervousness escalated to somatic symptoms of stomachaches, headaches, and lack of appetite. These ailments kept her home from school for days at a time. They also kept Shyla safe from uncomfortable situations and feelings of inadequacy.

When I met Shyla in her early 30s, she suffered from debilitating migraine headaches; anxiety had negatively impacted every aspect of her life. She had disconnected from friends, she had quit her job because she was overwhelmed, her marriage was suffering, and she felt she was failing as a mother. The anxiety that began as protection from the uncertainties of her life as a young child had now taken on the extreme role of keeping her from fully engaging in life.

Shyla's case is an example of anxiety as a personal burden. It developed out of her lived experiences. Parts took on anxiety to cope with what she could not control. Anxiety provided protection from challenging and uncomfortable situations as a child. However, over time, the parts went into overdrive and began protecting Shyla from what they perceived as having the potential of being difficult or causing harm. In this way the anxious parts kept Shyla from experiencing the deeper pain of not being enough.

Case Vignette 2: Anxiety as a Legacy Burden

The client, a 42-year-old single Black female named Annamarie, presented with extreme anxiety about finances. She questioned every financial decision she made. She worried about not having enough money to take care of her basic needs. She stressed about her business failing and becoming homeless. She felt shame around spending money and buying nice things, although she could afford them. She expressed concern about whether she was saving enough of her income "for a rainy day." She feared a financial future that was not reflective of her current financial situation.

Annamarie lived in an upper-middle-class neighborhood. She lived well within her means, saving over 50 percent of what she earned. But she still ruminated about losing her high-six-figure income as an online entrepreneur. As I learned more about Annamarie and saw how her worries were inconsistent with her current experiences, I became curious about her childhood as it related to money. Interestingly, she grew up in a middle-class family, attended private school, and didn't experience any financial hardships growing up. However, this line of questioning helped Annamarie remember her mother's constant worry about money and not wanting to spend it even though the family could afford it. Annamarie shared how she asked her mother for name-brand shoes or clothing and her mother scolded her, saying, "You should be ashamed of yourself for being so greedy and ungrateful" or "I can't believe you are this unappreciative." Annamarie shared that these conversations left her feeling unworthy and undeserving, as she knew they could afford what she was asking for.

Annamarie's mother had had a very different experience. She was raised by a widowed mother who struggled financially after the death of her husband left her raising five children alone. Annamarie's mother, the youngest of the five, didn't remember the prosperous times when her father was alive. Her memories were of struggle with barely enough to eat, bill collectors calling and coming to the house, her mother's exhaustion from working several jobs, and her never-ending money woes. So she impressed upon Annamarie the importance of saving instead of spending. She would say, "Annamarie, life can turn on a dime, and then where would you be?"

As Annamarie learned more about her parts, her compassion grew, and she realized that she responded to her vulnerable exiled part who felt unworthy the same way her mother responded to her requests for nice things. She doused the intensive feelings of unworthiness with harsh words of criticism.

With the exploration of Annamarie's family history and relationship to money, it became clear that her financial anxiety was a legacy burden. Annamarie had anxious parts about money, not because of her financial situation or her upbringing (personal burden) but because of the generational burden inherited from her mother and grandmother. And if it had been possible to speak with her grandmother, we might have discovered the legacy burden went further into the past.

As these two case examples demonstrate, personal and legacy burdens develop differently. However, the intention of the parts is the same: protection. With a personal burden, parts are protecting the system from previous pains experienced by the person. In the case of legacy burdens, the burdened parts are protecting the system from pains or traumas experienced within the generational line.

Which parts in the system carry legacy burdens—the managers, firefighters, or exiles? The answer is that any of these parts can inherit legacy burdens. Using Annamarie's story, let's see how this is possible.

Managers are burdened with responsibility and the need to control situations and outcomes. They vow to protect by not allowing the painful occurrence to happen again. Some of the ways managers accomplish their job are through people pleasing, criticizing, planning, caretaking, and overthinking. However, this list is not exhaustive.

Firefighters are burdened with repressing the pain of the exile. When the system feels the pain (fire) of the exile, firefighters put out the flame with distraction. They may use sex, drugs, food, dissociation, and self-harm to not feel the overwhelming emotions of the exile. Again, this list does not include all the ways a firefighter responds to the emergence of the exile. Exiles are usually young, vulnerable parts who have been wounded by trauma. They may be frozen in the time of the trauma and use extreme behavior to tell their story. When they express themselves, the person feels exposed and vulnerable and may experience shame. These are the feelings managers and firefighters are trying to keep hidden. Exiles seek redemption from what or who hurt them or from people or situations like the original trauma. To this aim, they may express dependency, openness, sensitivity, and anger.

Annamarie had an anxious part that worried about financial ruin, even though she was financially solvent with a successful business. The part that worried and ruminated about money is a manager. It keeps her focused on unseen possible future events to keep her from experiencing the pain of her exile. The anxious, worried part is a manager carrying the legacy burden.

The part that felt unworthy and undeserving of her mother's love is an exile. This part came to connect financial success and saving with love. The fear of financial ruin was intertwined with its overall sense of worth and being worthy of love. In working with this exiled part, we discovered that none of the unworthiness belonged to this part. All of it was a legacy burden, passed to Annamarie from her mother's feelings of unworthiness and shame about her own childhood experiences related to being poor.

Annamarie also had a firefighter who carried a legacy burden. The firefighter responded with criticism when the exile expressed feelings of unworthiness. The harshness that Annamarie's firefighter used to extinguish the intolerable feelings of unworthiness was inherited from her mother. Annamarie's firefighter part wasn't designed to be harsh but instead took on the harshness of her mother and used it to bring the system back into equilibrium when it was destabilized by the exile.

The case of Annamarie demonstrates how each type of part can be impacted by legacy burdens. Her manager carried the legacy burden of anxiety of financial ruin. Her firefighter responded to the expressed unworthiness of her exiled part with the legacy burden of harsh criticism. Lastly, her exile carried the legacy burden of unworthiness. Each of these legacy burdens was passed down on her maternal line from her mother's and grandmother's experiences and feelings connected to money.

Generational transmission is not limited to legacy burdens; legacy gifts are also inherited. Legacy gifts or heirlooms are inherent positive qualities passed down the generational line. This is evident in comments like "musical talent runs in the family" or "she has a calm presence like her great-grandmother." Legacy gifts are not taught or learned but innately woven into the fabric of a family, similar to the biological disposition of height or hazel eyes. However, when a person is carrying a legacy burden, the gifts are obscured. The healing of the legacy burden allows for access to the legacy gifts of the line. The case vignette that follows highlights the transformation of a cultural legacy burden into legacy gifts.

IFS CONCEPT 2: CULTURAL LEGACY BURDENS

The cultural legacy burdens of the United States defined in *Internal Family Systems Therapy* (second edition) are racism, patriarchy, individualism, and materialism. The foundation of the United States is built on stolen lands of Native Americans and the enslaved labor of stolen Africans. The founding of this country was based on the belief that Native Americans and Africans were inferior due to their race and therefore could be treated as less than a white person. Racism is oppression of a people based on race. Patriarchy is also traced to the beginning of our nation. The Founding Fathers are the white men instrumental in the forging of the United States. In our patriarchal society, power, control, and dominance are held by men. Individualism stresses self-reliance. As Richard Schwartz puts it, "Individualism fosters contempt for vulnerability and a belief that failure is a personal fault." Materialism focuses on gaining, maintaining, and achieving higher status.[2]

I see the impact of racism in my psychotherapy practice working with Black women. Many of my clients can be described as self-reliant and holding the Strong Black Woman legacy burden. This legacy burden is born out of the racist institution of enslaving African people. Writing in the psychology journal *Sex Roles*, researchers Martinque Jones, Keoshia Harris, and Akilah Reynolds describe the Strong Black Woman as emotionally restrained, independent, and a caretaker to others; they explain that that strength is viewed as psychological resistance to the prevalence of oppression in American society.[3]

My clients have shared experiences of horrendous injustices, demeaning abuses of their bodies, and painful losses with disconnection and lack of emotion. They tell these stories as if they happened to someone else.

They demonstrate the independence of the Strong Black Woman by not asking for help in overwhelming life situations and, furthermore, not even considering asking for help as an option. Clients have looked at me in disbelief when I ask them about seeking emotional or financial support or concrete aid. They meet my suggestion by insisting they're capable of doing it themselves; people would think them weak and unable to handle their business if they sought help. Or they explain that *they* are the person family or friends come to for help. This last response, justifying going it alone, is also a quality of the Strong Black Woman; she is a caregiver who puts the needs and even the wants of others before herself.

In the book *The Strong Black Woman,* Marita Golden outlines the experiences of Black women in the United States that contributed to the Strong Black Woman legacy burden:

> The Strong Black Woman was forged in the stinking, squalid hole of a slave ship, on the auction block, in an enslaved woman's ragged rush and run to freedom, nursing White babies instead of our own, when we were defined not really as "women," not like White women were, when it was asserted by Whites that because we were enslaved women we couldn't be "raped," when we were forced to work from dawn to dusk, and carry and bear the weight, fainting in the grip of "the spirit" in a pew on Sunday morning, becoming against the odds "the first Negro woman to_____," doing the grunt work of organizing behind the scenes for civil and human rights, training a White man who would take our job and then become our boss, standing shocked and silent at the news of

> the deaths of Trayvon Martin, Eric Garner, Sandra Bland, telling our daughters for the millionth time they have to be twice as good, basking in the acceptance and understanding of sister circles, where we are renewed, but where the cycle of adherence to the identity of the Strong Black Woman is also often reinforced.[4]

A woman who carries the Strong Black Woman legacy burden comes from a lineage of women who have had these experiences and transmitted them down the generational line, with the need to remain strong reinforced generation after generation by systemic racism and oppression. The legacy-unburdening steps in the vignette that follows were adapted from IFS senior lead trainer Ann Sinko.[5] I included ancestors in the unburdening process in a more active way, with a Well Ancestor actively releasing the burden and ushering in the gifts of the line.

Case Vignette 3: Strong Black Woman Legacy Burden and Gifts

Taren is a 36-year-old Black female therapist who presented for therapy overworked, burned out, feeling like she couldn't go on but wouldn't allow herself to stop. Her expressed goal for therapy was better time management skills. She believed with better skills she could accomplish her responsibilities without feeling drained.

She worked 60 or more hours a week as a rule. She was married with two children, ages 12 and 7. She owned a group practice with five employees and four social work student interns. She also carried a caseload of 15 to 20 clients. She held a leadership position in her local chapter of the National Association of Black Social Workers. She was the only caregiver to her ailing mother, whom she visited once or twice a week an hour's drive away. Taren complained of fatigue, dizziness, and off-and-on swelling of her legs. She attributed the symptoms to her busy work schedule, which was also the reason she gave for not having time to see a doctor.

I assessed the presence of the Strong Black Woman legacy burden when Taren shared the history of her mother, maternal and paternal grandmothers, and aunts. She described the women in her family as "getting things done because if they didn't, who would?" She comes from a line of women who worked hard, who didn't ask for help because that was a sign of weakness, and who valued being strong with the ability to press through exhaustion over their needs for rest and care. Taren agreed to explore the possibility that she had a legacy burden of being strong.

When I asked her where she noticed the need to be strong in her body, Taren answered, "It's all over, in every cell of my body and flowing through my blood."

When working with legacy, it is important to separate what portion of the burden is legacy and what is not. This is accomplished by determining the percentage of the burden that does not belong to you. So next, I asked Taren, "What percentage of this burden does not belong to you?"

Quickly and firmly she responded, "Eighty-five percent."

This means 85 percent of her need to be strong is a legacy burden, the percentage she absorbed from family and/or culture.

"Is there any reason for you to hold on to this burden?"

"Well, yes. I need to be strong to do what I need to do. What will happen to people who depend on me if I'm not strong?"

"I understand your concern; it makes a lot of sense. What if you could release the burden and remain productive in a way that doesn't cost you so much? Would you be interested?"

"Yeah, but I don't know how to do that."

"I can help you with it."

"Okay, then yes."

It is not unusual for parts to want to hold on to the Strong Black Woman legacy burden. This burden bonds the woman to other women in her family, it is part of her identity, and it serves as protection in an oppressive culture. To assist Taren in releasing this burden, I ask her to invite in any family members and ancestors who also carry this burden. It is important to invite in the Self-energy of these family members so they present in their highest state.

"Great, Taren, go on and invite in the Self-energy of your mother, grandmother, aunts, and any other family members and ancestors who you inherited this burden from, including those you do not know. Let me know when they're present."

Taren nods quietly, and after a moment says, "Okay, we're sitting in a circle."

"Now I'd like you to invite a Well Ancestor to come assist with the process."

"Do you mean someone who doesn't have this burden?"

"Yes, and well in other ways too."

"She's present, sitting in the middle of the circle."

"Good. How do you feel toward your family and ancestors?"

With tears streaming down her face, she says, "I love and appreciate them."

"Let them feel that energy from you."

Taren sits quietly nodding, looking around as if making eye contact with the women in the circle.

"Okay, Taren, focus again on where you notice the burden in your body. I want you to gather the burden from every cell and every drop of blood and give it to the ones you inherited it from and ask every woman to do the same: remove the burden from herself and give it to the ones she inherited it from."

After some silence, I continue, "When that process is complete, have the last person give the burdens to the Well Ancestor to release the burdens as she sees fit. You don't have to do anything; just watch the process, and let me know when it's done."

Taren is quiet for a few more minutes. Then she says, "The Well Ancestor collected the black tar-like sludge and buried it near a body of water, and a large shade tree grew on that spot."

"Okay, now ask the Well Ancestor to share the gifts of this line with you, your family members, and ancestors in whatever way she chooses."

In silence, tears slide from Taren's eyes again. Wiping her tears, she shares, "She showed me resting under the tree by the shore and told me I have the gift of knowing when to rest and resting without guilt. I am also gifted with the worthiness of my being and not my doing."

"Check in with your body and the places that held the burden. What do you notice?"

"I notice an openness. I feel more energetic. The part that was telling me I had to keep pushing is quiet."

"Very good. Let's have any parts that need to see the transformation join us. How do they respond?"

"They're surprised and like the new me."

"Good. Check in with the parts that released the Strong Black Woman legacy burden and see if they need anything else."

"Yes, they want me to remain connected to them."

"Good, see how they would like to remain connected."

She nods.

"Then show appreciation to your parts, family members, and ancestors for the work done today."

When I saw Taren two weeks after the legacy unburdening, she had made changes or had plans for changes in every area of her life. With her husband and children, she called a family meeting. She took responsibility for being ultra-self-reliant, not asking for help, and rejecting it when it was offered. Then she requested more support from them in the home going forward. With her mother, she explained she could no longer travel two hours round trip every week to oversee her care; instead, she offered several alternatives that involved her mother moving closer. At work, Taren came up with a plan to limit her load to 40 hours a week by no longer seeing clients, but instead focusing on managing the group practice and mentoring staff and interns. She also realized she has many capable, talented people on her staff to delegate tasks to. With the changes in her responsibilities at home and work, she turned her attention to her health and scheduled a doctor's appointment for the following month.

Taren shared that before the legacy unburdening, she put everyone and everything before herself. She described herself as being on "auto-pilot without an off switch." She said that being relieved of the burden provided clarity and gave her the much-needed space to make choices in her best interest without guilt instead of doing what she had always done.

You may have questions about the remaining 15 percent of Taren's burden, since she reported that 85 percent did not belong to her. The portion that was not a legacy burden was a personal burden, which we worked through in later sessions. It is possible for a burden to be partially from our lived experience (personal burden), inherited from our family or ethnic group (legacy burden), and absorbed from our culture (cultural legacy burden).

Meditation: Cabin with the Ancestor

This meditation was the first one given to me by the ancestors—the meditation I presented for the first time at the Black Therapists Rock Legacy Burden and Heirloom Summit. The meditation encourages a relationship between the listener and an ancestor. It supports releasing a long-held burden with the ancestor's support and receiving legacy gifts. This meditation can be used when a legacy burden has been identified or when a connection with ancestors would be useful in the healing process.

Relax and find a comfortable position to help your body settle.
Close your eyes if that feels right.
As you go inside, notice your body breathing.
Is it shallow and short or deep and long?
As you notice, see if you can lengthen and deepen each breath.

Imagine yourself in a lush green forest surrounded by your favorite trees, plants, and flowers.

As you explore the forest, a walking path appears before you. You take the path.

You walk until you come upon an overgrown patch that obstructs your view.

Curiously you part the brush to see what lies beyond.

A short distance away, you see a cabin.

The cabin beckons; as you get closer, you notice a welcoming warm glow inside.

Arriving at the door, you enter the cabin and find a wise ancestor seemingly waiting for your arrival.

If you arrive at the cabin and an ancestor is not present, take a few breaths and check and see if there are parts present preventing you from connecting with an ancestor.

If so, be with those parts and explore their concerns/fears about connection with an ancestor.

If there isn't a part with concerns, see if there are parts disappointed, surprised, hurt; be with those parts in the way they need you to be.

If an ancestor joins later, connect with them in whatever way feels good and right.

If an ancestor is present, you can join your ancestor on the floor.

Notice how happy your ancestor is to see you.

The ancestor tells you they have come to help you with a burden, one you have carried for some time.

They invite you to notice where in or around your body the burden is found.

They then instruct you to breathe into that place.

The ancestor compassionately opens their arms, encouraging you to give the burden to them.

If parts won't allow you to give the burden over, that's okay. Sit with those parts, asking about their fears and concerns.

If you are able, give the burden over in whatever way or portion that seems right.

As the burden leaves you, see what you notice.

Next, the ancestor hands you an ornately carved wooden box.

Opening the box, you discover gifts designed and chosen especially for you.

One by one, receive each heirloom into your body.

Consider how you will use your gifts in your life.

Once the embodiment is complete,
the ancestor says,
you are deeply loved,
you are whole,
you are the realization of my dreams,
and you are welcome to come back as often as you wish.

As you prepare to leave the cabin, offer gratitude and good-byes to your ancestor in a way of your choosing.

Exiting the cabin carrying the wooden box, you return to the forest path, retracing your steps.

Bring your awareness to your breath and breathe as you re-enter this moment and space. Slowly open your eyes when you're ready.

Exercise 1: Journal Capture

Journal what you would like to capture from this meditation, like a revelation, reflection, or anything significant you want to remember from this experience.

Exercise 2: Cabin with the Ancestor Journal Questions

After you've done the Cabin with the Ancestor meditation and written your quick Journal Capture, take some time to explore more deeply by responding to the following journal prompts.

1. What was your immediate experience and impression of your ancestor?
2. Where did you notice your burden?
3. If there is an image connected with the burden, draw it here.

4. Did you willingly give your burden to your ancestor? Why, why not?

5. What changes did you notice as you gave the burden away, if any?
6. What gifts did your ancestor give to you?
7. How will you use these gifts moving forward?
8. Will you continue a relationship with this ancestor? Why, why not?
9. If so, how?

Exercise 3: Understanding Your Legacy Burden

This exercise will help you to get to know and understand another part that carries a legacy burden.

What is the legacy burden?

Who in your family did you inherit this legacy burden from?

In the circle below, color in the percentage of this burden that does not belong to you.

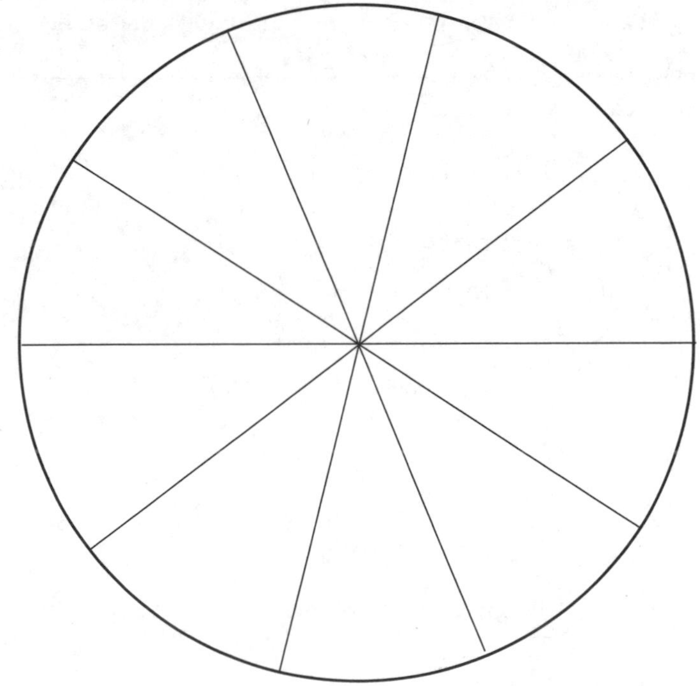

Where do you find this burden in or around your body?

Which parts carry the legacy burden?

Close your eyes and notice how you experience the legacy burden in your body.

What does it sound like?

What does it say?

How does it feel in your body?

What does it think?

What are its emotions?

If it shows as an image, draw it below.

What are the benefits of this legacy burden?

What is the cost of this legacy burden?

Complete this statement: "If I didn't have this legacy burden, I could . . ."

CHAPTER 12

Trailblazer

Integrating Unburdened Parts

The unburdening freed me. I feel like a brand-new girl. I no longer need to be tucked away and protected by Pricklee. Even though I'm still nine-year-old Tamala, I feel bigger, more lovable, and worthy. I feel connected to those around me instead of abandoned. I don't look to others to prove my worthiness. I am worthy because I exist. When I was hidden away, I felt physically small and unimportant. Releasing my burdens released my fears. I feel like I can do anything. I know I am not alone. Before, I didn't know there was someone to love me and to listen and understand. But now I love Tamala and she loves me. We have each other.

She came to me and asked what I want to be called now that I am free of my burdens. Up to that point, she referred to me as her younger self, the nine-year-old, and the exile. Those names no longer fit. With my gift returned, I placed my index finger at my closed lips, pointing upward, closed my eyes, and asked her and everyone inside to call me Shhhh. They, too, will need to place their finger at their lips with their eyes closed when they say my name, because it is both a sound and an action. I came here with the ability to sense things, and I am most sensitive to knowing when I get quiet. My name is a reminder to Tamala and the others that the best way to benefit from my gift and connect with me is in silence.

Pricklee was the biggest challenger to my transformation. When she first saw me after the unburdening, she appeared shocked and speechless. She stared, taking in my sparkly newness and confidence with disbelief. When she did speak, she said, "I feel like you don't need me. What will I do now? What if something unpredictable happens, then what? Will you need me to protect you then? I keep you and Tamala safe from hurting." I reassured Pricklee that I didn't need her to protect me. I let her know that I have something of value to benefit us all. Self informed Pricklee that she, too, could choose another role in the system since she didn't have to protect me in the same way.

Snapping her fingers, Pricklee said, "Just like that, I can choose a different job? I don't have to protect Shhhh any longer?"

"Yes, look at Shhhh. Does she appear to need your protection?"

"Well, no, but . . ." Her words trailed off.

"If you could choose to be or do anything you want, what would it be?" Self inquired.

"I know what I don't want. I don't want to be on high alert anymore. Constantly scanning for what could go wrong, course correcting to avoid unknown dangers, and reacting on autopilot with no control. I'm not sure what to do instead. I need time to think about it."

IFS CONCEPT 1: INTEGRATION

Our internal family is referred to as a system. The reason is quite apparent after a part is unburdened. When a change happens in one area of a system, other areas in the system have to adapt by changing in some way. Before an exile is unburdened, the internal system is kept in balance with managers and firefighters protecting the system and person from the pains of the exile. After unburdening occurs and the exile is transformed, the roles of protectors aren't necessary in the same way. Just as the exile takes on a new role in the system, protectors can do the same. A new type of balance is created through integration. The system needs to reorganize to accommodate new roles for parts. Integration occurs by bringing all the parts that were involved in the unburdening process to come and see the transformation of the newly unburdened part. The part that was once called an exile is now simply a part of the system. It is no longer referred to as an exile because it is no longer burdened and hidden away. The protectors of this part, the parts that expressed concerns or fears about Self connecting with the exile, and parts that had to unblend in order for the healing work to proceed are all called together to observe the changes in the unburdened part. This is done to see if these parts have any concerns about the transformation. Most often parts are accepting of the change. They may express surprise that the healing process worked, especially those parts that were skeptical. Protectors may share their concerns about their role now that it is apparent that their previous job is no longer necessary, or they may be concerned that the change won't last. As part of the integration process, Self will address the protectors' concerns. When the concerns of protectors are adequately addressed, protectors are invited to take on new roles within the system. The integration of changes in the internal system will translate to change in the external world, as the person will be less reactive to people and situations that previously caused activation or a trigger response.

This happens because the part that was exiled is no longer seeking redemption from people and situations like their trauma experiences. Instead of looking for validation of their worthiness and lovability, they can create genuine connections because they have released their burdens and can express the innate positive qualities they were born with before they became burdened.

With the changes in the formerly exiled part, protectors no longer need to respond proactively by controlling our lives to keep us safe from the pain of the exile or reactively extinguishing the pain once it's experienced. They can embrace their natural essence and take on a role in the system that reflects who they really are. Because the role protectors take on is a type of burden also. In most cases, protectors readily take on new roles after the unburdening of the exile. However, less frequently, complete integration requires healing of the protector. The healing process of a protector is the same as that of healing an exile. The protector will need witnessing and unburdening before it can take on a new role in the system.

IFS CONCEPT 2: INTENTION

Exiled parts have been hidden away for a long time and have held negative beliefs about themselves and/or the world for years. The transformation that happens with the unburdening of these beliefs requires reinforcement. This is accomplished by setting an intention with the recently unburdened part. We want to connect with this part daily for 30 days following the unburdening. The reason for the daily connection is to deepen the relationship between the part and Self, to help maintain the positive changes and new roles, and to decrease the chances of the part reverting to its old beliefs or becoming burdened again. We also need to check with the part to discover how it wants to maintain connection with Self. It may desire a particular type of interaction. We then make a commitment to honor the daily check-in and any ways the part wants to remain connected. This is the final step in the healing process.

IFS CONCEPT 3: UPDATING

Updating is a skill used when protectors believe you are the same age or close to the age you were when they took on their job of protection. Even though you are older, have taken on many responsibilities, and have had other life challenges and successes, these parts continue to view you as a vulnerable young child that needs their protection. We update parts by sharing with them what has happened in your life since whatever age or time they are stuck in. This can be accomplished by sharing images from various times in your life, playing the movie of your life for the part, or simply telling them. I've had clients offer photos from their life to support what they've told the part. An example of updating is shared in the case vignette that follows.

Case Vignette: The Replacement Child

Autumn is a Black woman in her early 30s with a thriving entrepreneurial business in the spirituality/self-care sector. She came to me for business coaching when she found herself stuck in analysis paralysis around expanding her business. She pursued each new idea with gusto. The problem was that new ideas were ever-present, which kept her chasing the newest one with no forward movement overall. She wavered between growing her current business and rebranding in a new direction.

As we worked with her system related to her business, we found three parts were involved in her indecision. She had a part that was anxious about changing what had been successful. Another part felt unworthy of success, so it created roadblocks to movement in a new direction. The third part felt resentment toward the anxious and unworthy parts for their indecision regarding business matters. It also felt resentment for the mistreatment of the exile part they all protected. We discovered this was an exile called The Replacement Child.

When the protector who was experiencing resentment was quite young, it learned that Autumn's mother had experienced the loss of another child before Autumn was born. As a young child, she believed it was her job to make her mother happy. She did not feel free to develop an identity separate from what her mother wanted or needed. However, she did not receive the attention she needed in return; she felt like an "afterthought." She was often left alone, which meant she had to figure things out by herself. She grew up feeling "insignificant and discarded." Although she lived in a household with extended family, no one seemed to have time for her. She noticed her family members were consumed with health, financial, and relationship problems. The Replacement Child was exiled to keep her and the system from the pain of feeling unworthy of love and attention.

When the protectors allowed access to the exile for healing, through witnessing, we learned The Replacement Child felt extremely lonely. She believed she was not a priority for anyone. She experienced her family from the perspective of an ignored observer, not a beloved member. When she did receive attention, she experienced it as what little they had "left over" and "never as a priority." She learned self-sufficiency out of necessity because when she sought attention or help, her family told her she was okay and brushed her away. This part needed someone to comfort and guide her. She didn't understand a lot about the lives of the adults she lived with. She was confused by their unwillingness to help her, and she was unprepared to handle the many tasks and decisions that were left to her.

Upon witnessing The Replacement Child's story, Autumn's Self offered the comfort, guidance, and validation she had needed long ago. Experiencing the calm, compassion, and connection of Self began the healing process for this part. She felt understood, which increased her trust of Autumn.

The burdens of The Replacement Child were aloneness, lack of connection, the need to pretend she was stronger than she was and knew more than she did, and the belief she was unworthy of care. After she was unburdened, she invited in the qualities of worthiness, connectedness, innocence, confidence, and an openness to try new things.

The integration step involved inviting the parts that felt anxious, unworthy, and resentful to see the transformation of The Replacement Child and take on new roles in the system. The anxious one expressed concern about this, while the other two recognized there was no need for continued protection and wanted to adopt new roles. Autumn spent time with the anxious one listening to its fears that "wildness" might be created within the system because the newly unburdened one would want to experience new things. It feared that in the quest for novelty, the newly unburdened part would become overwhelmed, the way she had as a child. With this information, I wondered if the anxious part knew that Autumn was an adult now. I asked Autumn to check.

"How old do you think I am?" Autumn asked the anxious part.

"Four," the anxious one answered.

Laughing, Autumn said, "I'm thirty." Then she said to me, "The part looks shocked."

"Ask the part if it would like to know what's happened in your life since you were four."

The part wanted to know, and Autumn chose to show highlights of her life in movie form. When that was complete, Autumn shared that the part expressed amazement about her accomplishments and how well she handled the many decisions in her life, both the joyous and the challenging ones. Once the part understood Autumn's capabilities, it was eager to relinquish its role of protecting her.

Integration involved the anxious one taking on the role of effortlessness. It wanted to bring ease in times of change and decision-making instead of anxiety and concern. The part that felt unworthy decided to transform into warmth, charm, and an inviting nature. The part that held resentment about Autumn's treatment as a child instantly released its resentment when it saw the other parts' transformation. Holding resentment for decades had been an exhausting burden, and this part chose to rest.

After the protectors took on new roles, Autumn's Self set intentions with The Replacement Child. The part wanted to remain connected to Autumn by bringing more freedom of choice into the system. She felt empowered to experience new things because she wanted to and not because she had no choice but to do them. Autumn agreed to check in with this part daily to see how she was doing and if she needed anything from her.

The changes in Autumn's internal system translated to changes in her decision-making abilities. Her protectors were free to act as advisors in decisions about the business. Their input was no longer motivated by the fear of a vulnerable part upsetting the system. Autumn described her internal transformation in one session this way: "My parts are quieter and calmer. I don't feel conflicted in my decisions. I have clarity I didn't have before. My parts trust me to decide, and instead of blocking me, they point out important things they don't want me to miss." Ultimately, Autumn and her parts decided on a both/and decision instead of an either/or. She decided to incorporate the best aspects of her current business with her new vision.

I want to note that once parts are unburdened, whether they are protectors or exiles, they are no longer referred to as protectors, managers, firefighters, or exiles—as you may have noticed while reading this chapter. They are simply parts. Although they may have names or qualities they prefer, they no longer carry the labels reserved for burdened parts in their extreme roles.

Meditation: Trailblazer

The Trailblazer meditation is the result of my therapy work with a few of my parts around being the first Black IFS lead trainer. I hadn't achieved the goal when I created the meditation, but I was in progress. Being the only or first Black person to (fill in the blank) was quite familiar to me; however, I had parts that pushed through and didn't allow me to attend to other parts who had insecurities and anxieties. IFS gave me the means to meet these parts and address their needs. The experience of getting to know my "Role Model" part gave birth to the Trailblazer meditation.

This meditation is useful when starting a new project or goal and setting intentions with newly unburdened parts.

Close your eyes or soften your gaze.

Adjust your body until it feels comfortable.

Notice how your body connects with the surface that supports you.

Inhale from the bottom of your feet, bringing the breath up through your body.

Exhale through your body and out the bottom of your feet.

Do that a few times.

Find yourself on the path of the new trail you're blazing.

As you walk this path, allow your senses to take in what's around you.

As you meander, you meet your eager, helpful parts.

Take time with them and learn what they want to share with you about this journey.

When your time with them is complete, you walk farther on the path, meeting your concerned and fearful parts.

Sitting with them, you listen curiously to their fears and concerns.

After your time with these parts, you travel your path until you come to a clearing.

In this clearing, you see qualities that will help you succeed on your path.

You sit with these qualities, listening to their wisdom about your path and how they may assist you.

These qualities encourage you to set intentions for your path.

Take as much time as you need to set clear intentions for moving forward.

Bring your awareness to your breath and breathe as you re-enter this moment and space. Slowly open your eyes when you're ready.

Exercise 1: Journal Capture

Journal what you would like to capture from this meditation, like a revelation, reflection, or anything significant you want to remember from this experience.

Exercise 2: Trailblazer Journal Questions

After you've done the Trailblazer meditation and written your quick Journal Capture, take some time to explore more deeply by responding to the following journal prompts.

1. What is the new path you're blazing?
2. How are your eager parts trying to assist you?
3. What's the message from your concerned or fearful parts?
4. What are the qualities you met in the clearing?
5. What intentions did you set?
6. How will these qualities assist you on your path?

Exercise 3: 30-Day Parts Check-In

Daily check-ins with newly unburdened parts are very important to the healing process. Use the following questions to connect with your part every day for 30 days after an unburdening.

How do you notice the part?

How do you feel toward the part? If it's other than a C-word, ask that part to unblend.

Check how the part is doing since the unburdening or since you last checked in.

What does the part want you to know?

Is there anything you want to share with the part?

Check if the part needs anything from you.

CHAPTER 13

Labyrinth with the Ancestor

A Self-Led Life

Self is who I am when parts are not blended with me. I express through the qualities of compassion, curiosity, calm, connectedness, confidence, courage, clarity, and creativity. When parts trust me, I can lead the system in a heart-centered, wise, intuitive manner. More than anything, I want to heal the wounded parts so they can return to their natural state, expressing their essential talents and gifts. They were never meant to carry these burdens, and I want to heal them by releasing them. I tend to lead with connection, compassion, and curiosity. Connection because I want parts to know they are not alone and that I care for them. Compassion because I want them to feel and know that I will not judge them. I have the capacity to hold their pain, no matter how great or enduring. Curiosity because I want to listen. I am open to hear as much as they want to share with me. I want to understand what they have gone through. I desire for them to experience being seen fully. Yet all of this is an offering; everyone inside has the choice to interact with me or not. I move at their pace and in their time.

I have created a Self-to-part relationship with each of my parts shared in this book. Remember Carefree, the part who took on the burden of pleasing others? She exiled and protected the part of herself who didn't feel valued and was told to change. Carefree did change, becoming what she thought others wanted her to be. Carefree trusted me to help the part of her that she exiled who felt not good enough in her natural state. When this part was healed, Carefree could release her compulsion to please others and express her innate qualities. Pleasing others became a choice instead of an obligation.

Antsy is another protector who was open to a relationship with me. She had been around for a very long time and created anxiety and panic related to success and achievement. She had a strong alliance with Perfection. These two parts protected an exile part who believed she was unlovable because she fell short of her father's expectations. After coming into relationship with me, both parts relaxed significantly. They allowed access to the exile, who released her burdensome beliefs. Antsy decided to keep her name but change her role to alert the system when we're taking on too much. She's the one who questions whether we need to take on new projects and/or responsibilities. Perfection was eager to release her burden too. She realized how stifling the pursuit of perfection was and that she never could achieve it. She embraced what her mother told her years ago and began to measure her progress and effort based on whether it was her best, recognizing that her "best" changes based on internal and external circumstances.

I learned a lot in building a relationship with Pricklee. Although there were other parts who did not understand what they viewed as her extreme irritation when she didn't get her way or the unexpected happened, her behavior made perfect sense once I heard her story. In fact, this was true for each of my parts. Once I learned how and why they took on their roles, their behavior was understandable. I also came to understand and appreciate that their roles were taken on when they were very young, with limited life experience, and they truly were doing the best they could.

I believe my relationship with Pricklee and Shhhh created the greatest internal shift. I say this because my intuition was heightened with access to Shhhh's innate intuition. Pricklee relaxed and began to trust Shhhh and me. As I continue to check in with both, intuition and knowing increase within my system. Pricklee has a new perspective about the unexpected. She no longer attempts to control things. She accepts that what is happening is exactly what needs to happen. Instead of bracing and attempting to control what she cannot, she brings calm and insight to these situations, and she leans in to the intuition of Shhhh to determine what needs to happen next. Often what's needed is time in quiet and stillness. Quite the opposite of how Pricklee responded in the past.

I was most enlightened by the parts that used my back injury to communicate with me. Parts came close to considering surgery as an option for the debilitating back pain I experienced that was still negatively impacting my life decades after the car accident I described earlier. When I learned that parts could use an injury or illness to express themselves, I became quite curious to know if this could be what was going on with me. It turned out that it was.

The change in the level of pain once I got to know the parts involved is nothing short of miraculous.

I discovered some parts were in the deepest denial of how much raising a child with special needs was impacting my family and my mental and physical health, while other parts kept pushing to find the right doctor, medicine, school, or program that would heal her. There were also parts who felt shame about how ineffective they were as a mother. When the internal chaos became unbearable, parts activated the pain centers in my lower back. This usually incapacitated me, requiring painkillers and bed rest, since I felt searing, shooting back pain any time I moved.

Once I came into relationship with the pain parts, I learned they were the response to the five-alarm fire going on inside. It took some time and many therapy sessions, but I was able to befriend the parts that felt denial, self-rage, rejection, and shame, and I was able to heal them. When this happened, the pain literally went away. I have been completely free of back pain since working with this coalition of parts.

In the chapter on polarization, we met Survive and Thrive. These parts were polarized around a decision to either close my private therapy practice and work full-time on becoming an IFS trainer or continue to juggle both. When Survive and Thrive gave me permission to heal the exile they protected who believed she was unworthy and unlovable unless she was achieving, they were able to give up their roles after she was unburdened. They have transformed from bickering adversaries to collaborative advisors, especially on decisions related to my business.

The last part to revisit is Cry Baby. Many parts within my system did not like the sensitivity of Cry Baby. They took on the voices of those in her life who admonished her tears and sensitive nature. In hearing Cry Baby's story, I came to understand that her sensitivity is a gift and is needed within the system. Being seen and valued for being herself encouraged her to release her burdens and reclaim her birthright. Her sensitivity is a type of wisdom. She has awareness and knowing that doesn't originate in her mind or brain, but through her senses and beyond. She feels and experiences the world, people, situations, and interactions deeply. Her view on crying has changed. She sees her tears as her superpower instead of her weakness. She is confident enough to express vulnerability in front of others and no longer apologizes for it. She believes by being comfortable enough to express her vulnerability openly, she gives others permission to accept and express their vulnerability too.

A question that often comes up, especially for folks who move through the world in Black and brown bodies, is, "How do parts remain Self-led if the external circumstances do not change?" There is an idea that if those external constraints still exist, protector parts will have to re-engage their extreme behaviors for protection. To explore this, let's go back to the vignette of Angel in Chapter 7. Her work environment did not change. Her boss continued to make racist comments and Angel endured daily microaggressions. She had to make a living, and although she did start looking for a new job outside her current organization, she did not find one during our time together. So how did her system cope?

When Angel's parts Go Along to Get Along, Bulldog, and the exiled part they protected were unburdened, her protectors took on new roles. Their roles involved them protecting her in Self-led ways instead of from a position of no choice. These parts helped Angel recognize she had a valuable skill set and encouraged her to reach out to a recruiter. While Angel waited for a new employment opportunity, these parts came to understand that they could not work hard enough, long enough, or take on enough extra work to change her boss's mind about people of color. So they stopped trying, which was a Self-led decision. Parts can still protect us without being the burdened protectors.

IFS CONCEPT 1: THE U-TURN

Outside of the core concepts of Self and parts, I have found the U-turn is one of the most powerful and beneficial concepts of IFS. A common response to parts becoming triggered is to blame the activation, discomfort, or upset on something or someone outside of ourselves. The U-turn gives us the opportunity to pause and see what's going on inside. When we get activated or triggered, we can U-turn by first noticing that we are triggered, and instead of blaming the situation or person for the activation, we can turn inward to see who got triggered and why. The activating event is probably similar to something hurtful or even traumatic from our past. Our parts respond to the activating event as if it were the same as that past event, or as if we were re-experiencing the actual event. It's only by making the U-turn that we give ourselves space to explore what is happening inside. The more access to Self-energy in a system, the easier it is to U-turn.

IFS CONCEPT 2: SELF-LEADERSHIP

Richard Schwartz and Martha Sweezy's classic text states that the goal of IFS therapy is to release parts from their extreme roles and beliefs to increase internal

Self-leadership, to achieve balance and harmony in the system, and to bring Self-energy to external systems.[1] For Self to lead, Self, not parts, must be in the seat of consciousness. Self-leadership happens readily when parts unblend. It is the natural result of parts releasing their extreme roles. Self-leadership opens the system to choose. Burdened parts do not have a choice. They act in their extreme roles out of necessity. Many parts aren't even aware of alternatives. When Self leads, it can *be with* parts; it can reparent them when needed and provide internal and external guidance. The only hindrance to Self-leadership is parts' inability or unwillingness to unblend. When parts unblend, Self naturally steps forward as the leader of the system. As parts come into relationship with Self and experience compassionate and confident leadership, they unblend more readily, further deepening their trust in Self to lead. Unburdened parts, whether they were in the role of protector or exile, now have increased access to Self-energy and can return to their natural state of being, creating balance and harmony in the system. A less burdened, balanced, harmonious, and Self-led system can interact with external systems in a Self-led way, bringing the qualities of Self (curiosity, confidence, creativity, clarity, compassion, connectedness, and calm) to each new interaction.

Case Vignette 1: Parts-Led Divorce

At age 42, Diane had two children ages 7 and 14 and her 20-year marriage was ending. She came to therapy to manage her rage. Her husband traveled out of state for work two weeks out of the month. She discovered that while he was away, he lived with another woman and the two young children he had with her. Diane's raging part spent consecutive sessions erupting and plotting to make him pay for what he did to their family. This rage part was polarized with a part that wailed for entire sessions and incapacitated Diane. She reported spending some days crying uncontrollably and some days plotting and carrying out vengeful actions against her husband. She had yet another part that wanted to report on all the things her husband did and continued to do that hurt her and the children. Diane had little access to Self-energy, so no matter what gains we made in session, they were lost between sessions.

Diane's raging, vengeful parts tried to discredit her husband to his boss, in their community and their church, and with their children. She withheld the children from visiting him until he was granted a court order, and even then, she didn't allow visitation until she was held in contempt of court. She accused him of being unfit, which brought Child Protective Services into their lives to supervise his visits until their investigation was completed. Ultimately, CPS ruled Diane's complaints that her husband was unfit were unfounded. Her raging parts were undeterred; in fact, they gained momentum.

When Diane's raging parts were most active, she canceled therapy sessions for weeks at a time. She would later share in session the irreparable financial, emotional, and property damage she was causing her husband. She also did everything she could to prolong the divorce proceedings. Diane's divorce was eventually granted, but her raging, vengeful parts did not stop. Eventually they turned their anger toward me and Diane stopped coming to therapy.

Case Vignette 2: Self-Led Divorce

Another client, Gemma, was getting a divorce because her husband had cheated on her. Gemma had parts that were sad and angry and "knew better." Gemma had suspected her husband's cheating for a few years and questioned him multiple times. Each time she asked, he denied it. Even though she couldn't prove it, she couldn't shake the feeling he was lying. Eventually she hired a private detective, who provided the proof in a few weeks: her husband was carrying on multiple affairs and had been for years.

Even though Gemma was new to IFS therapy, she had good access to Self. However, she had a Self-like part who wanted to "take the high road." Taking the high road initially seemed like a Self-led endeavor; however, after learning that the part wanted to prove Gemma was a good person, I understood it was a Self-*like* part. This part was polarized with the other three parts and believed that if those parts expressed themselves, Gemma would not be seen as a good person by her husband, her divorce attorney, or the judge. We discovered that this part's need to be seen as good had caused Gemma to accept poor treatment in her marriage, in friendships, and from family members.

Gemma was committed to her mental and emotional health. She attended sessions as scheduled, actively participated, worked with her parts outside of session, and completed all homework assignments. She even joined an IFS support group for women going through divorce.

We took time to get to know her sad, angry, "high road," and "knew better" parts. We discovered that the anger she thought was directed at her husband was really directed at herself because she didn't listen to the part that was certain of his cheating years ago. Gemma had parts who needed to trust his lies because they were afraid of starting over. She also had parts who thought of ways to hurt him or make him pay, but they never acted on these thoughts; it was more an expression of their anger. Ultimately, Gemma decided to focus on her parts and how what happened in her marriage was not an isolated incident. By coming into relationship with her protectors and unburdening the vulnerable parts, her system became more balanced, with Self leading. Gemma faced the divorce proceedings courageously, standing up for herself and confidently asking for what she wanted without needing to be seen as a good person.

Meditation: Labyrinth with the Ancestor

The Labyrinth with the Ancestor meditation is the eighth in the series given to me by my ancestors.

This meditation highlights the ways you've experienced Self-leadership and the qualities of Self-leadership in your life.

Bring your attention to your breath.

Notice how your breath moves in and out of your body.

Go inside by closing your eyes, softening your gaze, or whatever feels comfortable for you.

Visualize yourself walking in a garden. Take in the beauty in every direction. Feel the sun on your face and the fragrance in the air.

Walking deeper within, you see a tall semicircular hedge.

As you get closer, you recognize an Ancestor standing at a door-like opening in the hedge.

The Ancestor signals you to come with them.

The Ancestor says, "I have come to guide you through this labyrinth to remind you of the special gifts you carry within you."

They go on to explain, "Many people confuse a labyrinth with a maze. But unlike a maze, a labyrinth has no dead ends, and you cannot get lost. A labyrinth ends where it begins.

The Ancestor lets you know the experience of walking a labyrinth can be very tranquil and assures you that they will accompany you throughout.

You join the Ancestor inside to begin walking the outermost circle of the labyrinth.

As you walk together the Ancestor says, "The gift you possess is an inner wisdom consisting of eight qualities. I will ask you to recall examples from your life of how these qualities are already within you."

The Ancestor says the word *Compassion*, and right before your eyes you see a movie of the ways you have shown compassion to friends, family, people you love, strangers, and yourself.

The two of you walk the second circle, and the Ancestor says, "Creativity," and you see the novel ways you've found solutions to problems, examples of your unique self-expression, and your creative nature.

The Ancestor gently nudges you to continue walking the third circle and says, "Calm"; first notice your body and your breathing. Then you see images of times in your life when you were calm or brought calm to someone else. See if there were times when you were calm in a stressful or challenging situation.

When that is complete, the two of you move through the fourth inner circle, slowing your place a bit, and the Ancestor says, "Courage," and shows you how you have been courageous in small and not-so-small ways. How you have stood up for yourself or others.

Next you walk the fifth inner circle of Curiosity. The Ancestor shows you times from your life when you engaged others with genuine interest in the triumphs and challenges of their lives. Notice how your curiosity encouraged others to open to share with you.

Walking deeper into the labyrinth, the Ancestor says, "Confidence," and commences to show you examples of this quality from childhood to now.

The circles have gotten much shorter to walk. The Ancestor says, "Clarity," and you visualize the people and life situations when you knew exactly what to do or say without judgment.

You and the Ancestor arrive at the centermost part of the labyrinth, where you find a bench.

The Ancestor invites you to sit with them to watch how you have lived the final quality of Connectedness. You see connections from the past and the ones you have now. See if you can notice connections with other ancestors.

The Ancestor tells you it is time to travel back through the labyrinth and adds that you will discover tokens or gifts representing each quality of Self as you walk back to the beginning. The Ancestor goes on to say, "Each gift reflects how your qualities show up, and they are yours to take with you." The Ancestor hands you a container to collect your gifts.

Accompanied by the Ancestor, you look around this inner space for your token of Connectedness. When you find it, you place it in the container.

Walking the next circle, you find the Clarity token. Before placing it in the container, acknowledge why you selected it.

As you circle again, the gift representing Confidence is discovered, and you take it with you.

Walking around, you come across your Curiosity keepsake. Take note of your selection before putting it away.

Entering the next turn, you see the memento for Courage. Hold it in your hand; admire what it looks like.

The time to walk each circle increases as you locate and pick up the heirloom of Calm.

Next, you discover the Creativity gift.

Walking the outermost circle, you come upon the gift representing Compassion.

When the two of you arrive back at the entrance of the labyrinth, you both take time to admire the collected gifts of Self and their importance in your journey forward.

The Ancestor says, "Everyone has these qualities, but each person's expression of these gifts is unique. The most important thing about these gifts is you've always had them, and they are meant to be shared."

Take the time you need to end your time with the Ancestor, knowing you can meet with them whenever you please.

Bring your awareness to your breath and just breathe as you re-enter this moment and space. Slowly open your eyes when you are ready.

Exercise 1: Journal Capture

Journal what you would like to capture from this meditation, like a revelation, reflection, or anything significant you want to remember from this experience.

Exercise 2: Labyrinth with the Ancestor Journal Questions

After you've done the Labyrinth with the Ancestor meditation and written your quick Journal Capture, take some time to explore more deeply by responding to the following journal prompts.

What gift did you receive for each of the qualities of Self, and what is the significance of that gift?

1. Connection
2. Clarity
3. Confidence
4. Curiosity
5. Courage
6. Creativity
7. Calm
8. Compassion

Exercise 3: Create a U-Turn Statement

Use the eight qualities of Self to create a U-turn statement to remind you to go inside when you become activated by people, situations, and life circumstances. Below is my U-turn statement.

I am Confident that there are Creative ways to Connect inside to witness my parts with Clarity, while remaining Calm and being Courageous enough to stay Curious when my parts get activated, remembering that a little Compassion goes a long way.

CHAPTER 14

Still Listening

What happens after unburdening and healing the wounds of the past? We become less reactive to people and situations that previously triggered and activated our parts. One of my core childhood wounds was connected to rejection. A part of me felt rejected when my grandmother and aunts would not validate my experience by telling me the truth about the return address on the letter from my father. My feelings of rejection were further validated when I returned home from Louisiana to the truth of my parents' impending divorce. At nine years old I had a close bond with my father, and a part of me believed divorce meant a rejection of me and a loss of my connection with him. The feelings of rejection gained a stronger hold as life unfolded with my father's remarriage to a woman who had a child who got to live with him full-time, followed by the birth of their child, my younger brother. The part of me that felt rejected was exiled for over 40 years, and the reactivity of my raging protectors kept my father and me in a relationship that moved on a continuum from strained to estrangement for 11 years in my early adulthood.

For over 20 years I sought help through therapy, personal development workshops, retreats, and self-help books to heal this core wound of rejection. When I took the IFS Level 1 training, I had the opportunity to work with the parts of myself that felt both rage and rejection, and from that one demonstration session I knew IFS offered a level of healing that I had not experienced personally or seen professionally in my work with clients. I continued my IFS healing journey, and after unburdening each of my parts, protectors, and exiles who held the rage and feelings of rejection, I was able to engage with my father with no reactivity or triggering. Additionally, these parts were no longer triggered by other people and situations that reminded them of, or were similar to, my relationship with my father. In nine sessions, I received the elusive healing I had sought for decades.

However, my healing journey did not end with the parts that felt rage and rejection. I continued to discover other parts that held extreme beliefs. It seemed the more I worked with my system, the more willing parts were to come to the fore to receive the healing they witnessed other parts receiving.

This was most evident as I rose in leadership within the IFS Institute. I am the first Black person and person of color to enter the trainer track and be promoted to solo lead trainer. Being the first Black woman in a leadership role in an all-white organization activated distrusting, fearful, striving, and sad parts. Parts distrusted that the Institute would be true to their new stated mission of creating more inclusion and equity. Fearful parts were afraid I would be a tokenized checkbox for diversity. When the Institute put their mission into action by actively recruiting and training future leaders from the Global Majority and LGBTQIA+ communities, I had striving parts who wanted to be a good role model to those coming into the organization after me. Lastly, I had sad parts who were painfully familiar with blazing a trail alone with no road map as the first or only Black woman in a role.

I was committed to using the model to help me become a better leader and trainer. So each time a situation activated the parts I've just mentioned and I reached a point where I could not resolve the reactivity on my own, I went back to my highly skilled IFS therapist. This happened several times during the five years when I was taking on successive and expansive roles in leadership. Self wanted to bring healing to every part of me that was open to it. With each part that was healed, reactivity in my system decreased, while the expression of Self-energy increased. The increased access to Self-energy encouraged other parts of me to trust Self and the healing process. By the time I was in the training I described in the beginning of Chapter 4, I had immediate and reliable access to Self because of the relationship, trust, and connection with my parts.

PARTS STILL GET ACTIVATED

Working with and getting to know our internal system is an ongoing process. As we befriend, witness, and unburden parts, the system shifts. The increased trust and shifting opens us to deeper healing, uncovering new parts that want and need attention or parts we previously unburdened that need deeper healing. Either way, we still will get triggered or activated. Why does this happen? Well, we are not capable of being always Self-led. It would be akin to being in bliss or Nirvana constantly. But I have found that activation shows me where I have work to do. It points to the parts of me that need connection and healing. Admittedly, some of the work, especially with core wounds, deep trauma, and persistently distrustful parts can be difficult to do alone. Refer to the Resource section at the end of the book to locate additional resources and support.

GOALS OF PARTS WORK

I shared the goals of IFS therapy in Chapter 1, and I'll repeat them here. The goals of IFS therapy are to liberate parts from their extreme roles, restore Self-leadership, create balance and harmony within the system, and bring Self-energy to the external world.[1] Let's look at how reaching each of these goals results in a Self-led life.

Although I came to IFS first as a therapist and learner, then later as a therapy client, IFS is a guiding principle for my life. Now that my parts have an awareness and relationship with me and know they are not alone, they trust me to lead. However, their trust was earned. It was through listening to and validating their experiences that their confidence in Self increased. As parts released their burdens and embraced their gifts, the entire system has access to these natural gifts. I have fewer polarizations inside, which increases balance and a willingness for parts to work together, which in turn increases harmony. My parts welcome their roles as advisors and supporters who no longer have the burden of acting, feeling, and holding beliefs contrary to their innate nature. My parts readily unblend and allow for the U-turn when they get activated. As I've mentioned, I believe the U-turn is one of the most beneficial tools in IFS. The process of unblending with the knowledge that I am available and willing to be with their experiences has been life changing and life giving in my system. It gives my parts space to pause and let me

(Self) address the cause of their activation. I have learned that more than anything, my parts want acknowledgment and validation. They often need calming, as I have some excitable parts. My experience has been that no matter what my parts require, Self can and will provide it. IFS has transformed the ways I interact and engage with people, situations, and conflict both internally and in the world. I am present in ways I couldn't be before coming into a relationship with and healing parts of myself who had either no awareness or trust of Self.

BENEFITS OF PARTS WORK

As you have met, befriended, and even healed some of your parts, I hope you have already experienced the benefits of parts work. In working with our parts, we are not adding or gaining anything new; we are uncovering and increasing access to what we already possess. Below are nine benefits of parts work I have experienced and/or my clients have shared. I hope that you will also experience these benefits of your work.

1. Less parts reactivity: Parts become calmer when they have a relationship with Self and experience unburdening.
2. Greater choice: In their extreme states, parts have little to no awareness of other options beyond what they are currently doing. After unburdening, they have greater access to choose because they are free of their extreme roles and have access to their natural gifts.
3. Parts as advisors: The system has access to the wisdom of its parts. They can have an

active role, if they choose, in moving the system forward emotionally, physically, professionally, interpersonally, and in many other ways.

4. Improved relationships: With less reactivity, increased choice, and parts in new validating roles, relationships with other people improve. Parts can bring their positive qualities to relationships.
5. Trust in Self: Parts trust Self to lead the system and to assist them when they get activated because they have a firsthand experience of Self and the qualities that can help them transform.
6. Depersonalize behavior of others: We accept that everyone has parts, which means the poor behavior or mistreatment by others is not personal. We can see their parts in action.
7. Increased access to Self: The healing process naturally increases access to Self. As parts release burdens and extreme roles, they have more access to Self.
8. Grounded and present: With the release of extreme roles, the system is experienced as grounded and present.
9. Embodiment: The experience of feeling more "like yourself" or "present in your body" or "comfortable in your body." Also, a physical experience of the positive qualities parts express with the release of their burdens.

YOUR LISTENING JOURNEY

I have found that working with my parts and being in relationship with my ancestors is an ongoing process. I am committed to a long-term relationship with both. I continue to nurture these relationships, encouraging them to grow and deepen. Over time, the relationship with my parts has become more trusting, meaningful, and valuable. I have grown to lean in to the wisdom and guidance of my ancestors, especially when life doesn't seem to make sense. I appreciate their loving care for me and what is important to me, as shown in how they lovingly led me through many of the meditations shared here.

This book has been created as a joint project between me and the Writing Clan of my mother's mother's ancestral line. It has changed how I experience myself, the world, and how I interact with others. I have learned through this process that my ancestors are always present and available to me as I am for my parts. We, me, my parts, and my ancestors move through life connected and interrelated, no longer isolated and alone. I wish the same for you.

I encourage you to continue your healing journey by expanding and deepening your relationship with your parts and ancestors. Two key resources to assist you are locating an IFS therapist/practitioner and an Ancestral Lineage Healing practitioner. In addition to these resources, you'll find other unique and useful resources in the pages ahead.

Still Listening Resources

Author's Website

https://tamalafloyd.com/

IFS Therapy

Locate an IFS Therapist/Practitioner
https://ifs-institute.com/practitioners

Locate an IFS Therapist of Color
http://www.ifspoc.com

Locate a Multilingual IFS Therapist (languages available: Spanish, Portuguese, Mandarin, and Taiwanese)
https://ifstherapyonline.com/

Ancestral Lineage Healing

Locate an Ancestral Lineage Healing Practitioner
https://ancestralmedicine.org/practitioner-directory/

Jamari White, Ancestral Medicine Practitioner
www.kwawjamari.com

Ancestral Lineage Healing Courses
https://ancestralmedicine.org/online-course/ancestors/

IFS Training Programs

North American and International Programs
https://ifs-institute.com/trainings

Other IFS Courses

Queer and Trans IFS
https://www.qtifs.com/

Faith-based IFS course for Black Women
https://www.liberationlane.com/community

IFS Workshops and Retreats

IFS Institute
https://ifs-institute.com/news-events/events

Life Architect
https://lifearchitect.com/workshops/

Somatic IFS
https://www.embodiedself.net/

IFS-Based Recovery

Acqua Recovery
https://www.acquarecovery.com/ifs-internal-family-systems-inner-child-work

Path
https://www.path2recovery.org/

Latinx Healing Circles

https://view.flodesk.com/emails/647f87ab660ad5702615da40

IFS Scale

https://www.ifs-scale.com/

IFS-Related Books and Articles

Gessel, Nityda. *Embodied Self Awakening: Somatic Practices for Trauma Healing and Spiritual Evolution*. New York: W. W. Norton & Company, 2023.

Glass, Michelle. *Daily Parts Meditation Practice: A Journey of Embodied Integration for Clients and Therapists*. Listen3r, 2016.

Holmes, Tom, and Holmes, Lauri. *Parts Work: An Illustrated Guide to Your Inner Life*. Kalamazoo, MI: Winged Heart Press, 2007.

Kahler, Richard S., and Glass, Michelle. "The New Kid on the Block: IFS Informed Financial Therapy." *Journal of Financial Therapy* 14 (2023).

Kopald, Seth. *Self-Led: Living a Connected Life with Yourself and with Others. An Application of Internal Family Systems*. Exploration Services LLC, 2023.

Redfern, Emma, and Foot, Helen. *Freeing Self: IFS Beyond the Therapy Room*. B.C. Allen Publishing and Tonic Books, 2023.

Schwartz, Richard C. *Greater Than the Sum of Our Parts*. Louisville, CO: Sounds True, 2018.

Schwartz, Richard C., and Sweezy, Martha. *Internal Family Systems Therapy*, Second Edition. New York: Guilford Press. 2019.

Schwartz, Richard C. *No Bad Parts: Healing Trauma and Restoring Wholeness with the Internal Systems Model*. Louisville, CO: Sounds True, 2021.

Steege, Mary K., and Schwartz, Ricard C. *The Spirit-Led Life: Christianity and the Internal Family Systems*. CreateSpace Independent Publishing Platform, 2010.

IFS Books for Children

Jimenez-Pride, Carmen. *Emerson The Embodied Elephant*. Play Therapy with Carmen, 2023.

Patryas, Laura. *The 8 Superpowers Inside Me*. Independently published, 2023.

IFS Parts Cards

Eckstein, Sharon. *Inner Active Cards*. Lawton Michigan: Backwoods Press, 2018.

Jumanne-Marshall, Kenjji, Holmes, Tom, and Mirsky, Karina. *Black Experiences: Cards for Parts Work*. 2023.

Podcasts

Brown Girls Don't Do Therapy
https://www.instagram.com/browngirlsdontdotherapypodcast/

A podcast designed by a brown girl who happens to be a therapist to educate, empower, and support listeners to reconnect with their authentic selves. It explores how internal family systems (IFS) therapy or "parts work" can support people to find peace, harmony, and love in their life. This podcast is born from the need to break down the continued stigma of going to therapy in many BIPOC communities, and normalize that mental health *is* health. The host, Diviya Lewis, is a Registered Psychotherapist in Canada and a Certified IFS Therapist.

The One Inside: An Internal Family Systems
https://podcasts.apple.com/au/podcast/the-one-inside-an-internal-family-systems-ifs-podcast/id1460334766

The One Inside: An Internal Family Systems podcast is for anyone looking to find balance and harmony. IFS can help you understand the tug-of-war within your mind and rediscover your natural calm, creativity, and clarity. IFS can also heal the parts of you who hold pain.

IFS Talks
https://podcasts.apple.com/au/podcast/ifs-talks/id1481000501

IFS Talks is an audio series to deepen connections with the Internal Family Systems Model through conversations with lead trainers, authors, practitioners, and users.

The Financial Therapy Podcast
https://thefinancialtherapypodcast.com/

The Financial Therapy Podcast blends the nuts and bolts of financial advice with the emotions that drive financial decisions.

YouTube Channels

IFS Español: https://www.youtube.com/channel/UCehvJspi8LHMvh-mOpVp5mg

Self-Led Parenting: https://www.youtube.com/watch?v=OIWO_vbFEys

Free Download

Validation Parts Work with Self and Others
https://theshiftlesswanderer.com/the-practice-process-of-validation

Glossary

Ancestral lineage healing: A specific ritualized way to connect with wise ancestors to heal intergenerational trauma and reclaim and embody centuries of lost ancestral wisdom and guidance.

Befriending: Extending Self-energy to connect with a part to create a Self-to-part relationship and get to know the part.

Blending: When the feelings, beliefs, and energies of a part are in the seat of consciousness and block access to Self.

Burden: The extreme beliefs, thoughts, and perspectives parts take on because of trauma, attachment injury, and devaluing experiences.

Cultural burden: Negative beliefs, emotions, and energies of parts absorbed through interactions with the dominant culture and/or society.

Direct Access: Creating a Self-to-part relationship between the Self of another, usually an IFS therapist or practitioner, and your parts. Parts remain blended.

Do-over: A reworking of a traumatic experience in the presence of a compassionate witness. Also referred to as an emotionally corrective experience.

Exile: Typically, a young part who has experienced trauma and is kept out of awareness for fear that their pain will overwhelm the system.

Fears: Identifying and addressing the fears of parts that impede relationship building and/or healing.

Feel Toward: Noticing how you feel toward the part.

Find: Going inside to notice the part in or around your body.

Firefighter: A part who responds in extreme reactive ways when the pain of exiled parts is expressed or experienced by the system.

Flesh Out: Deepening the Self-to-part relationship with the part by extending increased Self-energy (the qualities of Self) and learning what the part wants to share about itself.

Focus: After finding the part, bringing awareness to the part to see what more you notice or experience.

Going inside: A turning of attention from the external to your inner world. This can involve closing your eyes, softening your gaze, looking downward, or simply sitting quietly and noticing what's happening inside of you.

In-sight: Creating a Self-to-part relationship between your Self and your parts. This requires the part to unblend or separate from Self.

Integration: The reorganization of the internal system to accommodate the new roles of parts after unburdening.

Intention: Commitments made between Self and parts to continue their relationship after an unburdening.

Internal Family Systems Therapy: A model of psychotherapy that holds that everyone has parts and a wise Self capable of healing and guiding your internal family of parts.

Invitation: Inviting essential qualities that were lost or obscured because of the burden the part carried prior to unburdening.

Legacy burden: Negative beliefs, emotions, and energies of parts passed down through familial and ancestral lines.

Legacy gift: Positive qualities of parts passed down through familial and ancestral lines. Also known as legacy heirlooms.

Manager: A part who responds in extreme proactive ways to keep you from experiencing the pain of exiled parts.

Part: A subpersonality you were born with who has feelings, thoughts, sensations, memories, speech, and many other qualities.

Personal burden: Negative beliefs, emotions, and energies of parts taken on because of their own traumatic and/or devaluing experiences.

Polarization: A relationship between two or more parts holding opposing views, beliefs, and behaviors.

Protector parts: Parts who have been forced into extreme roles to protect you and other parts due to trauma and/or devaluing life experiences.

Retrieval: An offer to bring a stuck or frozen exiled part out of a past trauma scene to a safe place of its choice.

Self: It is who you are when you are unblended from extreme parts. It is unaffected by past traumas, and it can heal them.

Self-leadership: When Self is in the seat of consciousness leading the system with wisdom, compassion, and intuition.

Self-like part: Manager parts who possess qualities like Self. They are empathic rather than compassionate and do not have the ability to heal the system.

Unblending: The process of a part separating from Self.

Unburdening: The process by which exiles and protectors release their burdens.

Updating: Sharing with parts what has happened in your life since the time where they are stuck or frozen.

U-turn: The pause to notice what is happening inside when activated and allowing space to unblend.

Witnessing: The beginning of the healing process for exiles, where they tell their story to a compassionate, curious, calm, and connected listener and witness.

Endnotes

Chapter 1

1. Richard C. Schwartz and Martha Sweezy, *Internal Family Systems Therapy* (New York: The Guilford Press, 2020).
2. Ibid.
3. www.kwawjamari.com
4. Ancestral Medicine, https://ancestralmedicine.org/.
5. Daniel Foor, *Ancestral Medicine: Rituals for Personal and Family Healing* (Rochester, VT: Bear & Company, 2017).
6. Richard C. Schwartz, *Introduction to the Internal Family Systems Model* (Oak Park, IL: Trailheads Publications, 2001).
7. Gina Ryder, "What Is Attachment Trauma?" *PsychCentral*, January 19, 2022.

Chapter 3

1. Richard C. Schwartz and Martha Sweezy, *Internal Family Systems Therapy* (New York: The Guilford Press, 2020).

Chapter 4

1. Richard C. Schwartz, *IFS Level 1. 8Cs Qualities of Self* [Training Handout] (Oak Park, IL: The Center for Self-Leadership, 2018).
2. Julia Sullivan, *IFS Level 1: 8Cs Worksheet* [Training Handout] (Oak Park, IL: The Center for Self-Leadership, 2018).

Chapter 8

1. John E. Sarno, *The Mindbody Prescription: Healing the Body, Healing the Pain* (New York: Warner Books, 1998).
2. David Schechter, *The MindBody Workbook: A Thirty Day Program of Insight and Awareness for People with Back Pain and Other Disorders* (Culver City, CA: MindBody Medicine Publications, 1999).
3. Richard C. Schwartz and Martha Sweezy, *Internal Family Systems Therapy* (New York: The Guilford Press, 2020).
4. Ibid.

Chapter 9

1. Pam Krause, *IFS Level 2 Deepening and Expanding. Hope Merchant Steps* [Training Handout] (Oak Park, IL: IFS Institute, 2022).

Chapter 11

1. Ann L. Sinko, "Legacy Burden," chapter, in *Innovations and Elaborations in Internal Family Systems Therapy*, eds. Martha Sweezy and Ellen L. Ziskind (New York: Routledge, 2016).
2. Richard C. Schwartz and Martha Sweezy, *Internal Family Systems Therapy* (New York: The Guilford Press, 2020).
3. Martinque K. Jones, Keoshia J. Harris, and Akilah A. Reynolds, "In Their Own Words: The Meaning of the Strong Black Woman Schema among Black U.S. College Women," *Sex Roles* 84, no. 5–6 (June 20, 2020): 347–59, https://doi.org/10.1007/s11199-020-01170-w.
4. Marita Golden, *The Strong Black Woman: How a Myth Endangers the Physical and Mental Health of Black Women* (Coral Gables, FL: Mango Publishing, 2021).
5. Sinko, "Legacy Burden."

Chapter 13

1. Richard C. Schwartz and Martha Sweezy, *Internal Family Systems Therapy* (New York: The Guilford Press, 2020).

Chapter 14

1. Richard C. Schwartz and Martha Sweezy, *Internal Family Systems Therapy* (New York: The Guilford Press, 2020).

Index

A

B

C

D

E

F

G

M

N

P

R

S

T

U

V

W

Y

Acknowledgments

The most important person I want to thank is my husband, Ernest Floyd, for taking this amazing journey with me. I would have been lost without his tech-savvy support—ensuring adequate Internet speed, recommending and updating various applications, filming and editing my marketing video, supporting my vision, and loving my many parts who showed up along the way. He gave me the space I required to write and made sure we had plenty of fun, lightheartedness, and adventure too.

Thank you to Dr. Richard Schwartz for creating the IFS model and generously sharing it with the world, even in times of challenge and doubt. I am grateful to Dr. Schwartz for encouraging my desire to become an IFS trainer and author and supporting my growth, through his teachings and by working with my system and parts. I also appreciate his words of encouragement to deepen my relationships with my ancestors.

To Sarah Stewart, Psy.D., my IFS therapist, who has been my rock through this process. She has met and worked with many of my parts shared in this book and has supported my healing and Self-leadership journey. Her support has been invaluable.

I want to acknowledge three IFS senior lead trainers who guided, taught, and supported my process: Chris Burris, LMFT; Pamela Krause, LCSW; and Ann Sinko, LMFT.

Chris Burris greatly impacted my development as an IFS solo lead trainer. He mentored me in such a generous fashion, sharing his knowledge and experience while highlighting my strengths and providing tools and suggestions for my growing edges. From the beginning, Chris supported my idea of writing a book about IFS and including ancestor-inspired meditations. He was invaluable in my understanding and application of the model and translating that knowledge into this book.

Pam Krause is a gem of a teacher and friend. During the mentoring process and beyond, I have been so fortunate to benefit from her 20-plus years of experience. Pam helped me truly embrace the qualities of Self that I witnessed her exemplify—especially her unmatched gift of speaking for her parts. Pam's willingness to share her vulnerability gave my parts not only permission but a road map for expressing themselves. Under Pam's guidance I learned the powerful healing effect of Self-energy.

I am grateful to Ann Sinko for her contribution to expanding my understanding of legacy burdens and the gift of ancestor work with IFS. As one of my mentors, Ann helped me learn the nuances of the model. Once I understood the model, she helped me appreciate its intricacies, which broadened and deepened my experience with IFS.

I want to thank the entire Hay House publishing team who assisted in bringing this book forth. I am most grateful to Anne Barthel, Executive Editor, the woman who journeyed the entire distance with me. As a new writer, Anne was exactly the editor I needed, because she made sure I understood the process at every single step. Most importantly, she had a way of delivering corrective feedback that didn't activate my critical, perfectionist parts. I am immensely grateful for the many thoughtful suggestions she made to improve my writing. I learned from Anne that writers write and editors edit. I'm grateful for our partnership and how beautifully she edited my work.

Thank you, Devon Glenn, for improving the readability of my work with your copyediting. Simple changes made a world of difference. I'm glad to be the beneficiary of your talent.

Monica O'Connor, who assisted Anne, asked great questions that expanded my ideas for the book and clarified concepts for readers new to IFS.

I am grateful to Allison Janice, senior acquisitions editor, who first reviewed my meditation audio proposal. When we met, she simply asked if I'd be open to writing a book and expanding on the audio idea. Thank you, Allison, for asking the question that honored my ancestors' intentions and opened the way for *Listening When Parts Speak*.

About the Author

TAMALA FLOYD, LCSW, is a psychotherapist, IFS lead trainer, consultant, author, and speaker with over 25 years of experience. She received a master's degree in social work from the University of Southern California and an undergraduate degree in psychology from California State University–Long Beach. She has taught at the University of Phoenix and the University of Southern California in human services and social work. Her work focuses on women's trauma, mothering, and relationship issues, helping women identify and heal emotional wounds that impede their success and coaching them in achieving fulfilling life goals.

tamalafloyd.com

Hay House Titles of Related Interest

YOU CAN HEAL YOUR LIFE, the movie,
starring Louise Hay & Friends
(available as an online streaming video)
www.hayhouse.com/louise-movie

THE SHIFT, the movie,
starring Dr. Wayne W. Dyer
(available as an online streaming video)
www.hayhouse.com/the-shift-movie

***

ANCESTORS SAID: 365 Introspections for Emotional Healing by Ehime Ora

CONNECTED FATES, SEPARATE DESTINIES: Using Family Constellations Therapy to Recover from Inherited Stories and Trauma by Marine Sélénée

HAPPY DAYS: The Guided Path from Trauma to Profound Freedom and Inner Peace by Gabrielle Bernstein

TRANSFORMING THE MOTHER WOUND: Sacred Practices for Healing Your Inner Wise Woman through Ritual and Grounded Spirituality by Monika Carless

YOU'RE GOING TO BE OKAY: 16 Lessons on Healing After Trauma by Madeline Popelka

All of the above are available at your local bookstore, or may be ordered by contacting Hay House (see next page).

***

We hope you enjoyed this Hay House book. If you'd like to receive our online catalog featuring additional information on Hay House books and products, or if you'd like to find out more about the Hay Foundation, please contact:

Hay House LLC, P.O. Box 5100, Carlsbad, CA 92018-5100
(760) 431-7695 or (800) 654-5126
www.hayhouse.com® • www.hayfoundation.org

Published in Australia by:
Hay House Australia Publishing Pty Ltd
18/36 Ralph St., Alexandria NSW 2015
Phone: +61 (02) 9669 4299
www.hayhouse.com.au

Published in the United Kingdom by:
Hay House UK Ltd
The Sixth Floor, Watson House,
54 Baker Street, London W1U 7BU
Phone: +44 (0) 203 927 7290
www.hayhouse.co.uk

Published in India by:
Hay House Publishers (India) Pvt Ltd
Muskaan Complex, Plot No. 3,
B-2, Vasant Kunj, New Delhi 110 070
Phone: +91 11 41761620
www.hayhouse.co.in